Nature and Madness

OTHER BOOKS BY PAUL SHEPARD

Man in the Landscape: A Historic View
of the Esthetics of Nature

The Subversive Science: Essays toward the Ecology of Man,
edited with Daniel McKinley

Environ/Mental: Essays on the Planet as a Home,
edited with Daniel McKinley

The Tender Carnivore and the Sacred Game

Thinking Animals: Animals and
the Development of Human Intelligence

The Sacred Paw: The Bear in Nature, Myth, and Literature,
with Barry Sanders

The Others: How Animals Made Us Human

Traces of an Omnivore

The Only World We've Got

Nature and Madness

PAUL SHEPARD

Foreword by C. L. Rawlins

The University of Georgia Press

Athens & London

Published by the University of Georgia Press
Athens, Georgia 30602
© 1982 by Paul Shepard
Foreword © 1998 by the University of Georgia Press
All rights reserved

The paper in this book meets the guidelines
for permanence and durability of the
Committee on Production Guidelines for Book Longevity
of the Council on Library Resources

Printed in Canada

98 99 00 01 02   P   5 4 3 2 1

LIBRARY OF CONGRESS CATALOGING IN PUBLICATION DATA

Shepard, Paul, 1925–
Nature and madness / Paul Shepard ;
with a foreword by C. L. Rawlins.
p.   cm.
Originally published: San Francisco : Sierra Club Books, c1982.
Includes bibliographical references and index.
ISBN 0-8203-1980-5 (pbk. : alk. paper)
1. Nature—Effect of human beings on. 2. Human ecology.
I. Title.
GF75.S53 1998
304.2—dc21   97-23869

BRITISH LIBRARY CATALOGING IN PUBLICATION DATA AVAILABLE

for Jane, Kent and Margaret,
Who have demonstrated in their epigenesis
How the gen can repair the epi
And the epi summon the gen

Contents

Foreword

C. L. Rawlins

Paul Shepard's introduction, written in 1982, places this work in its intellectual context: the analysis of human character as a natural phenomenon. But his ideas also have tremendous moral weight. Despite our present environmental destructiveness, he says, we are capable of being good, not just as individuals but as a species.

Of his many distinguished books, Shepard believed *Nature and Madness* to be the most important, for its presentation of what amounts to a unified field theory of the human condition. To support this, he draws from a stunning array of disciplines. His research in the fields of biology, genetics, zoology, anthropology, psychology, ethology, history, theology, poetics, and myth is deployed not to demonstrate his intellectual powers, grand as they are, but because all these are necessary components of human ecology, a field of study that he practically founded.

Shepard began the work that led to *Nature and Madness* in the 1960s, when such thinking was a brave and lonely enterprise. He helped organize key conferences, attracting thinkers such as John Cobb Jr., John Rodman, Garrett Hardin, William Leiss, John Lilly, John Livingston, Joseph Meeker, Roderick Nash, Vine Deloria Jr., Gary Snyder, and George Sessions, whose work would inform both philosophy and science. And he edited two books, with Daniel McKinley, that collected the most provocative writing in what would later become known as environmental studies: *The Subversive Science: Essays toward an Ecology of Man* (1969) and *Environ/Mental: Essays on the Planet as Home* (1971).

Yet my appreciation for *Nature and Madness* comes not out of esteem for the scholarship, fine though it is, but because the book has become part of my life. I read it with a thrill of recognition. More than any other single work, *Nature and Madness* illuminates my past, confirms my present, and assures me, in the deepest way, that I belong to this world. As Shepard wrote in an early essay titled "Ecology and Man—A Viewpoint": "Ecological thinking . . . reveals the self ennobled and extended rather than threatened, as part of the landscape and the ecosystem. . . . We must affirm that the world is a being, a part of our own body."

As far back as I can remember, I felt like this. More than being in church, I loved the junipers. In the outdoors I learned how ants move cookie crumbs and how the first drops of rain sound, raising the dust. Since this fascination felt, to a western Mormon child, like a form of rebellion, I also learned to lie about the dirt on the knees of my pants and, soon thereafter, to regret the lie. Some of my guilt arose from the fact that I seemed to trust such things—junipers, ants, rain, dust— more than anything I was told.

The first gift I received from *Nature and Madness* was the realization that my instinct ran true. I was doing what a healthy human child must do, in order to grow. Left to myself, I roamed compulsively, discovering where ants built the biggest hills, where horned lizards could be caught, and where wild mint grew. Then my father would take a new job and our family would move, and I would begin my explorations again.

In the natural world, as Shepard writes, "There is no end to what is to be learned." But my teachers stayed inside. And more than anything else, school was confinement. We sat in hard chairs, in dull rooms of brick, while outside rain fell and flowers bloomed. I felt guilty slipping away but could not stop myself. Remorse was easily outdistanced as I hiked the burning flats and found overhangs from whose shade I could watch the desert. In the canyons, cottonwood leaves rattled in the breeze as clouds bloomed overhead, trailing their cool shadows. In the desert, you can smell the rain before it falls, and the odors of juniper, piñon, and sage are like skeins of color, braiding in the air.

I needed a teacher—an elder—who could speak of such things, but my scout leaders did not care for walking or learning the names of plants. Instead, they gave orders: chop wood, build fires, pitch tents. We would find a spot and colonize it. After doing as I was told and no more, I would steal off, intent on pursuing my coyote education.

The gap—between what I was told and what I knew—was profound. And so, the second gift I received from *Nature and Madness* was the realization that the distance was not of my making: it came from being human, Mormon, western, and American. What I felt was the strain of trying to connect two things—nature and culture—that did not connect. They had at one time, perhaps, but that was past.

I wanted to be outdoors, and more—I needed to be. Since my forebears were farmers and ranchers and engineers, being outdoors meant work. So between bouts with education, I bucked bales and herded sheep and then joined the Forest Service to scrub toilets and fight fires. It was good to sleep beneath canvas and spend whole days under the changing sky. Thus, I lived two lives. A season of work paid for a quarter or two in school—shoved into hot rooms and stuffed with rules, chronologies, and procedures. It was a relief to take off for the next dead-end job. Education was the opposite of outdoors.

But it should not be the opposite. First, we need to roam and learn from nature itself. To dabble, wade, dip, wallow, and splash. Toss pebbles, or pick them up. Put a smooth stone on your tongue. Examine your face in a pool. Sleep by the river until it sounds in your dreams. *Then,* study hydrology.

The human learning curve, traced over a million years, is not easily redrawn. And the process is individual. You must do your own developmental work in the natural world. It cannot be fulfilled in a classroom, nor by reading books, nor by watching films: these are supplements, not food itself. Just as we live through our bodies, it is this natural bounty—fresh experience—that the child brings back to the human circle: *Mommy, look! Daddy, come see!*

If the gift is denied—*Where have you been? You soiled your dress! Is your homework finished?*—an injury is done. If the wounding is frequent, the child will be angry, frightened, lonely, scarred.

Leaving childhood, Shepard writes, you enter a time of testing, from which you should emerge as an adult, at home in the world. Yet if you have not been filled, by both nature and culture, you will fail. Being ingenious and adaptable you may construct the necessary world in thought, and it may serve. But you will be caged in yourself and fearful of the otherness outside.

The place of understanding is not necessarily kind. Heaven and earth meet there, and they will crush you if you do not hold them apart, so you need resolute strength, like the hardness of old cowboys. But such strength, unrelieved, will also crush you, so you need lightness and trickery and music. Nature is fire and ice and gravity, falling rocks and rushing streams, but it moves as well through myth and poetry: voices, sounding through the smoke.

My growing up came late. In July 1973, mostly by chance, I went to the Salt River Range in Wyoming with Mitchell Black, three dogs, a string of horses, and a herd of sheep. In the mountains, nature worked its ancient way with me. When we returned in late September with the snow, I'd taken my place in the world. The sad part is that this occurred mostly through struggle and resistance on my part. If I had kept to the sidewalks and mown fields, and played known games by the rules, the fullest portion of my life would never have taken place.

With the onset of biological maturity, we feel the same thing: the land's deep imprint. Yet, as our lives take on a manufactured sameness, most frequently we lack the raw material—and it must be raw—for this vital passage. Any arrested human act—a meal broken off, an unfinished poem, *coitus interruptus,* an aborted pregnancy—provokes a kind of organic anger. And so it is, Shepard writes, with the stalled development that accompanies modern culture—we feel a bone-deep fury, one we discharge through fanatical belief, unending war, and the accelerating destruction of our world.

For Paul Shepard, this idea—that mass culture draws collective power from blocking individual development—was the result of broad study and prolonged thinking. His search across many disciplines is rare in the present atmosphere of diverging studies and narrowing conclusions. But his thoughts compare with the best work now being done in all these fields.

On the importance of seeing ourselves as a species, he reasons that we are constituted by millions of years of ecological development. That is, we are not souls apart from bodies, nor are we souls and bodies apart from earth. At the heart of this book is the fact that there is no possible substitute we can devise for growing up in the natural world. This is where Shepard breaks from the scholarly herd: from the Platonic esteem for logic above rocks and twigs, from the Cartesian insistence on character as a blank slate, and from the Puritan reverence for bodiless intent.

As biologist Edward O. Wilson writes: "The green prehuman earth is the mystery we were chosen to solve." And just as we have built cities we cannot inhabit, we may also have devised lives we can no longer live. In this pass, wisdom may consist not so much of learning bright new tricks as of keeping our old ones intact.

Nature taught me what every good coyote learns. Water is wet. Rocks fall. Rain turns to snow. But every year there are fewer rocky coverts to explore and fewer streams from which to drink. So, in perverse proportion, we require more nature books and field institutes.

I teach, sometimes. I don't promise wisdom or oneness. Those are profound aims, and private ones. Instead, we will learn to do something: map a stream and measure the flow. You will discover slippery rocks, bottomless silt, mosquitos. You might fall in, *whoops,* and then get chafed, hiking out in wet shorts. You might feel bored, uncomfortable, uneasy—or vaguely happy, without knowing why.

Or you might have an awakening. In *Nature and Madness,* Shepard calls this sudden, luminous connection "a biological heritage of the deep past." While the event may be sudden, most of all it takes time. You have to sprout in darkness and bud against the frost, then flower—take the risk of beauty—in order to bear fruit. But if you are ripe, it may not matter whether you do field science, go on a Crystal Vision Quest, or herd sheep, as I once did. And this fruit, maturity, is the yield of human life.

Nature and Madness is, above all, a sensible book. You do not have to stop believing in the rocky integrity of our world in order to accept yourself. And this is the fatal flaw, as Shepard describes it, in our current state of belief. To embrace the mass religions or ideologies of the present, we must first deny what we know in our very bones: how the world works. And this denial, this halt, this dead stop in our development wreaks spiritual havoc: as Goya put it, the sleep of reason breeds monsters. Or as Shepard writes, "The only society more fearful than one run by children, as in Golding's *Lord of the Flies,* might be one run by childish adults."

But this tendency to harm is not, as we are often taught, the result of inherent evil, but rather the progressive failure of customs and institutions to allow our growing up. We behave like thwarted infants—smashing and grabbing—because we feel that way.

I remember my last year in high school, drinking rum in the parking lot of J.B.'s Big Boy on Las Vegas Boulevard. We got out of the car, four of us, and put our shoulders to a wall of cinder blocks and toppled it into the neighboring yard, then laughed and drove away. I remember our walking on empty railroad tracks through the desert and coming on a switch, being somehow infuriated by the red steel diamond bolted to it and cursing it as one, prying up rocks and empty bottles to smash against it, and then ripping it from the rusty iron upright with bare hands. We bore it off like a prize.

Madness is a form of power. Imagine, then, the collective power to be gained by spurring this adolescent fury, prolonging it, harnessing it with ideologies and armies, or turning it against the land, to raise pyramids, cathedrals, concrete dams.

It was only after reading *Nature and Madness* that I grasped our fundamental Western myth: the Garden of Eden, and an angry God casting us, male and female, out. The biblical motif—forbidden fruit, knowledge of good and evil—is both tantalizing and obscure. Freud's interpretation, discerning the Father's hidden desire for his daughter, Eve, and her pact with the serpent in order to escape with Adam, cuts somewhat closer to the bone. But Shepard's analysis, that the very idea of a single Father for all creation—monotheism—brought about our psychic exile from the garden of the world, is profound, indeed, and fearful in proportion.

This is the wrenching human difficulty posed by *Nature and Madness:* that we must, for the most part, accept our lives as being in some way blocked and stunted, see ourselves as less than we intend. There is no intellectual balm for this.

Yet it is no more forbidding than the otherness a Lakota youth faced, hungry and scared in his vision pit, dug against looming space; no more daunting than the gravity an Apache girl felt, a real body racing up a real mountain, frightened, breathless, into womanhood.

Given the depth of our predicament, Shepard offers a curiously hopeful diagnosis: we can still grow up. Despite all, we can learn how the world works and learn to be good animals, not fallen angels. We have not lost the ability, which is innate, but only missed the chance.

That possibility is the third and greatest gift I received from Paul Shepard, though I stumbled into growing up ten years before *Nature and Madness* appeared. Nor did I find the book until ten years after it was published, in 1993 on a remainder table in Moab, Utah. I was on a reading tour for a book of my own, short on cash, but was struck by the title. I read the first few pages, and it would not let me go. Reaching home, I dug for the old black journal that had gathered dust for twenty years and traced how, in 1973 in the Wyoming mountains, I'd finally done that lovely trick encoded in our genes. In retrospect, my life—stubborn, feral, and contrary—made sense. It was like seeing a deer, dark eyes fixed on me, where an instant before I'd seen only brush and rock, a confusion of light and shade.

I sent a grateful note to Shepard in care of Pitzer College, California, and enclosed a copy of my book, *Sky's Witness*. A letter came back from the other end of my home county in Wyoming: he and Florence Krall, writer and professor at the University of Utah, had a cabin there. He praised my book and invited me to visit. But by the time I worked up the courage to call, they had left Wyoming for the winter.

Meanwhile, I had another book to write. In 1994, I returned to the Salt River Range to walk the old trails. By then the book had a title, *Broken Country*, and I realized how much it owed to Shepard. I wrote to Shepard, asking if I might dedicate it to him. He called to say yes, but he and Florence were leaving, so we postponed dinner once more.

In November, Florence wrote that Paul had been diagnosed with inoperable cancer. He had family and close friends, I thought, and former students who should see him. Having no such claim, I sent a sheaf of poetry. Florence wrote from Salt Lake to say that they were reading the poems, and that they seemed to help.

In autumn 1995 we had that long-awaited meal. Paul looked tired, but we sat with glasses of whiskey by the cabin window and talked about what we could see, the darkening willows and frosted grass. Florence looked sorrowful and strong. She had made bread, and the smell of it filled the house. After we ate, Paul signed a copy of *Thinking Animals* and gave it to me.

Despite illness, Paul was faithful to his work. A new book showed up in the mail, *The Others: How Animals Made Us Human*, signed, "In friendship, Paul Shepard." I stayed up late reading it and we talked on the phone. In June 1996 he was hoping to make it up to the cabin, but Florence said he lacked the strength. My own *Broken Country* was completed. It would do him good to see it, she said. I asked the publisher to rush, and he held the bound proof the week before he died.

If you count the time we spent face to face, I knew Paul Shepard for one full day. But I read his books, a life distilled. He was a scholar, through and through, while I will never be, but we found a quick accord. My ragged living confirmed his hard-won thoughts. And this curious symbiosis resolved some doubts on either side: his, perhaps, about devoting his life to scholarship; mine at having fled universities for the pure charm of the earth.

We write to make ourselves known and to give up what we have learned, and risk ourselves to those ends. While I risked my neck, and accomplished only what countless human beings have done before, Paul Shepard has given us something entirely new. He risked following his thoughts, like a hunter on a spoor, no matter where they led, and reached a profound understanding. In *Nature and Madness,* he addresses the theme of loss that runs like an aquifer beneath all our conscious discourse, but which has never been articulated this clearly, and with such good sense.

In *Nature and Madness,* Shepard explains what we suffer from and why. Unshielded by myth or jargon, he explores the most dangerous human terrain, the yearning in which our beliefs all find their origins. His genius is to refute their narrowness and cruelty, while confirming their right, and ours, to exist.

Instead, he returns us to the beauty that we might have been, and that ancient, pathological event, our departure from the world our bodies knew.

———————

C. L. Rawlins was born and still lives in the windblown state of Wyoming with Linda Baker Rawlins, a librarian and former backcountry ranger. A writer and field hydrologist, Rawlins is president of the Wyoming Outdoor Council. His books include *A Ceremony on Bare Ground, Poems; Sky's Witness: A Year In the Wind River Range;* and *Broken Country: Mountains and Memory.* Rawlins's forthcoming books include *Mountain Streams: Notes and Revelations* and a collection of poems, *In Gravity National Park.*

Preface

THIS IS A PROGRESS REPORT. Initially my effort was
to seek and understand the historical origins of an environmental esthetic. In *Man in the Landscape* I examined Renaissance sources of the American traditions of landscape painting and gardening as kernels from which our leisure takes its
expression in travel and nature study. But that esthetic is too
fragile and wayward to bear much of an ecological ardor. Its
failure is due to the time dissonance of evolution and ideas.
Culture, in racing ahead of our biological evolution, does not
replace it but is injured by its own folly. Beginning again, in
The Tender Carnivore and the Sacred Game, I sought a more durable model for ourselves in the deep history of ancestral hunter-gatherers. In an unexpected way I was rewarded, for foraging is a more thoughtful activity than I knew. I felt that I had
glimpsed a central figure of consciousness, whose expressions
in intelligence and speech appeared to be bound in each
individual human emergence, as well as in that of the whole
species, to plants and animals. I attempted to trace that emergence in *Thinking Animals*. Meanwhile, the sense of a normative psychogenesis became a compelling idea, of development
as an organ. The prospect of general, culturally-ratified distortions of childhood, of massive disablement of ontogeny as
the basis of irrational and self-destructive attitudes toward the
natural environment is the prospect to which I now turn.

Most of my teachers I never met, nor am I sure, given my

xix

thesis, that they would assent heartily to my apprenticeship. Nonetheless, I revere their work and this book comes from a cross-reading of the psychology of human development by such masters as Erik Erikson, Peter Blos and Jerome Kagan, of religious history as explored by Joseph Campbell and Mircea Eliade. Certain writings have been particularly seminal: Homer Smith's *Man and His Gods,* Anthony Storr's *The Dynamics of Creation,* and Herbert Schneidau's *Sacred Discontent.* Both I and my students have found Joseph Chilton Pearce's *Magical Child* to be a beautiful and provocative statement of the lifelong effects of the non-human environment on the newborn. Especially rewarding have been the papers, books and personal encouragement of Harold F. Searles.

Hervey Kleckley's discussion of the fluidity of typologies in psychopathology in *The Mask of Sanity* warned me that I should avoid clinical diagnoses, that such terms as schizoid and paranoid might indicate a mode but, for a non-physician like myself, not an etiology.[1] His idea of the mask, the enactment of normalcy which enables psychopaths to hide behind the routines of daily life, emboldened me to think that pathology might be epidemic in a culture, yet hidden from itself. All of these authors stimulated my curiosity about the relationship of the complex course of child development and its deformities to those 'external' environmental problems which we so often interpret either as a minority conceit or a momentary administrative awkwardness.

I am grateful to Malcolm Wood for his scrutiny and criticisms, to Sierra Club Books editor James Cohee for his diligent help and editorial conscience, to Robin and William Matthews who remind me with much energy that to become too categorical about Christianity is to enact the dualism of which it is accused, and to Joseph Meeker, who made valuable suggestions for improvements of several parts of the manuscript. My wife, June Shepard, as always, has been a resolute critic of vagueness and carelessness. A Humanities Fellowship from the Rockefeller Foundation helped make time possible for reconnaissance of the relationship of ecology to the history of thought.

Like so many other ideas that seem at first original, this one turned out not to be private property. I soon found that Erich Fromm had already asked "Can a society be sick?" in *The Sane Society*. He assailed sociological and cultural relativism, wryly observing that consensual validation has no bearing on mental health: "That millions of people share the same forms of mental pathology does not make these people sane" —a remark as urgent and valid as when it was written twenty-five years ago.

The subject thrust me sideways so to speak, into the field of psychohistory. In my remedial purview I found that most psychohistory has been concerned with the biographies of famous men. Closer to Fromm's view is the work of Kenneth Keniston and Lloyd deMause. Keniston says, "Largely ignored so far in the study of historical change have been the emerging concepts of developmental psychology—a small but rapidly growing body of theories about the sequences of stages of human development, the conditions that foster or inhibit development in children, and the consequences of early development for adult roles, symbolizations, and values . . . Historical or cultural conditions which may stimulate development in one sector of life may well fail to stimulate it or actually retard it in other sectors . . . Some societies may 'stop' human development in some sectors far earlier than other societies 'chose' to do so."[2]

DeMause observes that "child-rearing practices are not just one item in a list of cultural traits. They are the very condition for the transmission and development of all other cultural elements, and place definite limits on what can be achieved in all other spheres of history." His "psychogenic theory of history" is a documentation of immense abuse of children, so that one wonders whether there ever have been good parents. Indeed, his book begins, "The history of childhood is a nightmare . . ." But DeMause's "history" only goes back a millennium or two and does not leave the precincts of the Western world. His work supports the contention of this book—that there are profound psychic dislocations at the root of modern society—but he offers for comparison no archetype, no healthy paradigms in real human groups.

I am encouraged by several anthropological friends to think, on the contrary, that there have been and are societies in which a demonstrable affection for children is manifest in loving concern and a benign strategy of appropriate, age-grade care that fosters their growth toward maturity and the capacity for wisdom and mentorship. Some examples are the Manus of New Guinea, the Crow and Comanche of North America, the Aranda of Australia, and the !Kung San of Africa. From this perspective of phylogenetic felicity we start, pausing to remark that herein are speculations for which I do not apologize, except to say: Reader take note; this book is by an amateur and is based on informed conjecture.

1

Introduction

—

MY QUESTION IS: why do men persist in destroying their habitat? I have, at different times, believed the answer was a lack of information, faulty technique, or insensibility. Certainly intuitions of the interdependence of all life are an ancient wisdom, perhaps as old as thought itself, occasionally rediscovered, as it has been by the science of ecology in our own society. At mid-twentieth century there was a widely shared feeling that we only needed to bring businessmen, cab drivers, housewives, and politicians together with the right mix of oceanographers, soils experts, or foresters in order to set things right.

In time, even with the attention of the media and a windfall of synthesizers, popularizers, gurus of ecophilosophy, and other champions of ecology, in spite of some new laws and indications that environmentalism is taking its place as a new turtle on the political log, nothing much has changed. Either I and the other "pessimists" and "doomsayers" were wrong about the human need for other species, and the decline of the planet as a life-support system, or our species is intent on suicide—or there is something we overlooked.

Such a something could be simply greed. Maybe the whole world is just acting out the same impulse that brought a cattlemen's meeting in West Texas to an end in 1898 with the following unanimous declaration: *"Resolved,* that none of us know, or care to know, anything about grasses, native or otherwise, outside the fact that for the present there are lots of them, the best on record, and we are after getting the most out of them while they last."[1]

But it is hard to be content with the theory that people are bad and will always do the worst. Given the present climate of education, knowing something about grasses may *be* the greedy course if it means the way to continued prosperity.

The stockmen's resolution seems to say that somebody at the meeting had been talking new-fangled ideas of range management. Conservation in the view of Theodore Roosevelt's generation was largely a matter of getting the right techniques and programs. By Aldo Leopold's time, half a century later, the perspective had begun to change. The attrition of the green world was felt to be due as much to belief as to craft. Naturalists talking to agronomists were only foreground figures in a world where attitudes, values, philosophies, and the arts—the whole weltanschauung of peoples and nations—could be seen as a vast system within which nature was abused or honored. But today the conviction with which that idea caught the imagination seems to fade; technology promises still greater mastery of nature, and the inherent conservatism of ecology seems only to restrain productivity as much of the world becomes poorer and hungrier.

The realization that human institutions express at least an implicit philosophy of nature does not always lead them to broaden their doctrines. Just as often it backs them into a defense of those doctrines. In the midst of these new concerns and reaffirmations of the status quo, the distance between earth and philosophy seems as great as ever. We know, for example, that the massive removal of the great Old World primeval forests from Spain and Italy to Scandinavia a thousand years ago was repeated in North America in the past century and proceeds today in the Amazon basin, Malaysia, and the Himalayan frontier. Much of the soil of interior China and the uplands of the Ganges, Euphrates, and Mississippi rivers has been swept into their deltas, while the world population of man and his energy demands have doubled several times over. The number of animal species we have exterminated is now in the hundreds. An uncanny something seems to block the corrective will, not simply private cupidity or political inertia. Could it be an inadequate philosophy or value system? The idea that the destruction of whales is the logical outcome of Francis Bacon's dictum that nature should serve man or René Descartes' insistence that animals feel no pain since they have no souls seems too easy and too academic. The meticulous analysis of these philosophies and the discovery that they articulate an ethos beg the question. Similarly, technology does not simply act out scientific theory or daily life flesh out ideas of progress, biblical dogma, or Renaissance humanism. A history of ideas is not enough to explain human behavior.

Our species once did (and in some small groups still does) live in stable harmony with the natural environment. That was not because men were incapable of changing their environment or lacked acumen; it was not simply on account of a holistic or reverent attitude, but for some more enveloping and deeper reason still. The change began between five and ten thousand years ago and became more destructive and less accountable with the progress of civilization. The economic and material demands of growing villages and towns are, I believe, not causes but results of this change. In concert with advancing knowledge and human organization it wrenched the ancient social machinery that had limited human births. It fostered a new sense of human mastery and the extirpation of nonhuman life. In hindsight this change has been ex-

3

plained in terms of necessity or as the decline of ancient gods. But more likely it was irrational (though not unlogical) and unconscious, a kind of failure in some fundamental dimension of human existence, an irrationality beyond mistakenness, a kind of madness.

The idea of a sick society is not new. Bernard Frank, Karl Menninger, and Erich Fromm are among those who have addressed it. Sigmund Freud asks, "If the development of civilization has such a far-reaching similarity to the development of the individual and if it employs the same methods, may we not be justified in reaching the diagnosis that, under the influence of cultural urges, some civilizations—or some epochs of civilization—possibly the whole of mankind—have become neurotic?" Australian anthropologist Derek Freeman observes that the doctrine of cultural relativism, which has dominated modern thought, may have blinded us to the deviate behavior of whole societies by denying normative standards for mental health.

In his book *In Bluebeard's Castle*, George Steiner asks why so many men have killed other men in the past two centuries (the estimate is something like 160 million deaths). He notes that, for some reason, periods of peace in Europe were felt to be stifling. Peace was a lassitude, he says, periodically broken by war, as though pressures built up that had little to do with the games of national power or conflicting ideologies. He concludes that one of those pressures found its expression in the Holocaust, motivated by unconscious resentment of the intolerable emotional and intellectual burden of monotheism. Acting as the frenzied agents for a kind of fury in the whole of Christendom, the Germans sought to destroy the living representatives of those who had centuries ago wounded the mythic view of creation, stripping the earth of divine being and numinous presences, and substituting a remote, invisible, unknowable, demanding, vengeful, arbitrary god.

Steiner's approach to these seizures of extermination as collective personality disintegration has something to offer the question of the destruction of nature. What, in Steiner's framework, is indicated by the heedless occupancy of all earth habitats; the physical and chemical abuse of the soil, air, and water; the extinction and displacement of wild plants and animals; the overcutting and overgrazing of forest and grasslands; the expansion of human numbers at the expense of the biotic health of the world, turning everything into something man-made and man-used?

To invoke psychopathology is to address infancy, as most mental problems have their roots in our first years of life and their symptoms are defined in terms of immaturity. The mentally ill typically have infantile motives and act on perceptions and states of mind that caricature those of early life. Among their symptoms are destructive behaviors that are the means by which the individual comes to terms with private demons that would otherwise overwhelm him. To argue with the logic with which he defends his behavior is to threaten those very acts of defense that stand between him and a frightful chasm.

Most of us fail to become as mature as we might. In that respect there is a continuum from simple deprivations to traumatic shocks, many of which are fears and fantasies of a kind that normally haunt anxious infants and then diminish. Such primary fantasies and impulses are the stuff of the unconscious of us all. They typically remain submerged or their energy is transmuted, checked, sublimated, or subordinated to reality. Not all are terrifying: there are chimeras of power and unity and erotic satisfaction as well as shadows that plague us at abyssal levels with disorder and fear, all sending their images and symbols into dreams and, in the troubled soul, into consciousness. It is not clear whether they all play

5

some constructive part in the long trail toward sane maturity or whether they are just flickering specters lurking beside that path, waiting for our wits to stumble. Either way, the correlation between mental unhealth and regression to particular stages of early mental life has been confirmed thousands of times over.

The passage of human development is surprisingly long and complicated. The whole of growth through the first twenty years (including physical growth) is our ontogenesis, our "coming into being," or *ontogeny*. Dovetailed with fetal life at one end and adult phases at the other, ontogeny is as surprising as anything in human biology. Anyone who thinks the human creature is not a specialized animal should spend a few hours with the thirty-odd volumes of *The Psychoanalytic Study of the Child* or the issues of the *Journal of Child Development*. In the realm of nature, human ontogeny is a regular giraffe's neck of unlikely extension, vulnerability, internal engineering, and the prospect of an extraordinary view from the top.

Among those relict tribal peoples who seem to live at peace with their world, who feel themselves to be guests rather than masters, the ontogeny of the individual has some characteristic features. I conjecture that their ontogeny is more normal than ours (for which I will be seen as sentimental and romantic) and that it may be considered to be a standard from which we have deviated. Theirs is the way of life to which our ontogeny was fitted by natural selection, fostering a calendar of mental growth, cooperation, leadership, and the study of a mysterious and beautiful world where the clues to the meaning of life were embodied in natural things, where everyday life was inextricable from spiritual significance and encounter, and where the members of the group celebrated individual stages and passages as ritual participation in the first creation.

This seed of normal ontogeny is present in all of us. It

6

triggers vague expectations that parents and society will respond to our hunger. The newborn infant, for example, needs almost continuous association with one particular mother who sings and talks to it, breast-feeds it, holds and massages it, wants and enjoys it. For the infant as person-to-be, the shape of all otherness grows out of that maternal relationship. Yet, the setting of that relationship was, in the evolution of humankind, a surround of living plants, rich in texture, smell, and motion. The unfiltered, unpolluted air, the flicker of wild birds, real sunshine and rain, mud to be tasted and tree bark to grasp, the sounds of wind and water, the calls of animals and insects as well as human voices—all these are not vague and pleasant amenities for the infant, but the stuff out of which its second grounding, even while in its mother's arms, has begun. The outdoors is also in some sense another inside, a kind of enlivenment of that fetal landscape which is not so constant as once supposed. The surroundings are also that-which-will-be-swallowed, internalized, incorporated as the self.

The child begins to babble and then to speak according to his own timing, with the cooperation of adults who are themselves acting upon the deep wisdom of a stage of life. At first it is a matter of rote and imitation, a naming of things whose distinctive differences are unambiguous. Nature is a lexicon where, at first, words have the solid reality of things.

In this bright new world there are as yet few mythical beasts, but real creatures to watch and to mimic in play. Animals have a magnetic affinity for the child, for each in its way seems to embody some impulse, reaction, or movement that is "like me." In the playful, controlled enactment of them comes a gradual mastery of the personal inner zoology of fears, joys, and relationships. In stories told, their forms spring to life in the mind, re-presented in consciousness, training the capacity to imagine. The play space—trees,

7

shrubs, paths, hidings, climbings—is a visible, structured entity, another prototype of relationships that hold. It is the primordial terrain in which games of imitating adults lay another groundwork for a dependable world. They prefigure a household, so that, for these children of mobile hunter-gatherers, no house is necessary to structure and symbolize social status. Individual trees and rocks that were also known to parents and grandparents are enduring counterplayers having transcendent meanings later in life.

In such a world there is no wildness, as there is no tameness. Human power over nature is largely the exercise of handcraft. Insofar as the natural world poetically signifies human society, it signals that there is no great power over other men except as the skills of leadership are hewn by example and persuasion. The otherness of nature takes fabulous forms of incorporation, influence, conciliation, and compromise. When the juvenile goes out with adults to seek a hidden root or to stalk an antelope he sees the unlimited possibilities of affiliation, for success is understood to depend on the readiness of the prey or tuber as much as the skill of the forager.

But the child does not yet philosophize on this; for him the world is simply what it seems; he is shielded from speculation and abstraction by his own psyche. He is not given the worst of the menial tasks. He is free, much as the creatures around him—that is, delicately watchful, not only of animals but of people, among whom life is not ranked subordination to authority. Conformity for him will be to social pressure and custom, not to force. All this is augured in the nonhuman world, not because he never sees dominant and subordinate animals, creatures killing others, or trees whose shade suppresses the growth of other plants, but because, reaching puberty, he is on the brink of a miracle of interpretation that will transform those things.

8

He will learn that his childhood experiences, though a comfort and joy, were a special language. Through myth and its ritual enactments, he is once again presented with that which he expects. Thenceforth natural things are not only themselves but a speaking. He will not put his delight in the sky and the earth behind him as a childish and irrelevant thing. The quests and tests that mark his passage in adolescent initiation are not intended to reveal to him that his love of the natural world was an illusion or that, having seemed only what it was, it in some way failed him. He will not graduate from that world but into its significance. So, with the end of childhood, he begins a lifelong study, a reciprocity with the natural world in which its depths are as endless as his own creative thought. He will not study it in order to transform its liveliness into mere objects that represent his ego, but as a poem, numinous and analogical, of human society.

The experience of such a world is initially that the mother is always there, following an easy birth in a quiet place, a presence in the tactile warmth of her body. For the infant there is a joyful comfort in being handled and fondled often, fed and cleaned as the body demands. From the start it is a world of variation on rhythms, the refreshment of hot and cold, wind like a breath in the face, the smell and feel of rain and snow, earth in hand and underfoot. The world is a soft sound-surround of gentle voices, human, cricket, and bird music. It is a pungent and inviting place with just enough bite that it says, "Come out, wake up, look, taste, and smell; now cuddle and sleep!"

There is a constancy of people, yet it is a world bathed in nonhuman forms, a myriad of figures, evoking an intense sense of their differences and similarities, the beckoning challenge of a lifetime. Speech is about that likeness and unlikeness, the coin of thought.

It is a world of travel and stop. At first the child fears being left and is bound by fear to the proximity of his mother and others. This interrupted movement sets the pace of his life, telling him gently that he is a traveler or visitor in the world. Its motion is like his own growth: as he gets older and as the cycle of group migrations is repeated, he sees places he has seen before, and those places seem less big and strange. The life of movement and rest is one of returning, and the places are the same and yet always more.

Now the child goes to the fringes of the camp to play at foraging. Play is an imitation, starting with simple fleeing and catching, going on to mimic joyfully the important animals, being them for a moment and then not being them, feeling as this one must feel and then that one, all tried on the self. The child sees the adults dancing the animal movements and does it too. Music itself has been there all the time, from his mother's song to the melodies of birds and the howls of wolves. The child already feels the mystery of kinship: likeness but difference.

The child goes out from camp with adults to forage and with playmates to imitate foraging. The adults show no anxiety in their hunting, only patience; one waits and watches and listens. Sometimes the best is not to be found, but there is always something. The world is all clues. There is no end to the subtlety and delicacy of the clues. The signs that reveal are always there. One has only to learn the art of reading them.

There is discomfort that cannot be avoided. The child sees with pride that he can endure it, that his body profits by it so that on beautiful days he feels wonderful. He witnesses sickness and death. But they are right as part of things and not really prevalent, for how could the little band of fifteen continue if there were dying every day?

The child is free. He is not asked to work. At first he can climb and splash and dig and explore the infinite riches about him. In time he increasingly wants to make things and to understand that which he cannot touch or change, to wonder about that which is unseen. His world is full of stories told, hearing of a recent hunt, tales of renowned events, and epics with layers of meaning. He has been bathed in voices of one kind or another always. Voices last only for their moment of sound, but they originate in life. The child learns that all life tells something and that all sound—from the frog calling to the sea surf—issues from a being kindred and significant to himself, telling some tale, giving some clue, mimicking some rhythm that he should know. There is no end to what is to be learned.

At the end of childhood he comes to some of the most thrilling days of his life. The transition he faces will be experienced by body and ritual in concert. The childhood of journeying in a known world, scrutinizing and mimicking natural forms, and always listening has prepared him for a whole new octave in his being. The clock of his body permits it to be done, and the elders of his life will see that he is initiated. It is a commencement into a world foreshadowed by childhood: home, good, unimaginably rich, sometimes painful with reason, scrutable with care.

Western civilized cultures, by contrast, have largely abandoned the ceremonies of adolescent initiation that affirm the metaphoric, mysterious, and poetic quality of nature, reducing them to esthetics and amenities. But our human developmental program requires external models of order—if not a community of plants and animals, then words in a book, the ranks and professions of society, or the machine. If the ritual basis of the order-making metaphor is inadequate, the world can rigidify at the juvenile level of literalism, a boring place, which the adult will ignore as repetitive or exploit as mere substance.

In connecting ecological havoc to warpings of this ontogeny, I must also describe where I think such a healthy ontogeny should lead. I suspect I risk losing the whole case here: there are so many thoughtful portraits of maturity that I am bound to omit someone's criteria. My cues come from four men, none of whom can be blamed for my own knobby *bricolage.* I am captivated first by Erik Erikson's vision of a growing, clarifying sense of identity as the ultimate psychological goal of all the vicissitudes of infant, childhood, and adolescent passage making. Erikson sees the tasks of this sifting and differentiating as a meeting ground of heritable and experiential parts (together composing an epigenetic pattern) of the first two decades of life, not only leading to a heightened consciousness of personal uniqueness, but as the basis of the individuated personality itself. He sees ontogeny as a series of emergent tasks or critical-period concerns whose specific processes rise and fall in their intensity as surely as scenes in a drama, yet overlap like feathers on a bird. The successful traverse of Erikson's age-specific quest themes is essential.

To this idea of development as a crescendo of more detailed separateness Harold F. Searles has described in detail a vital counterplay: the concurrent growth of a conscious and unconscious web of connectedness analogous to the spread of kinship ties in human groups. Identity is not only a honing of personal singularity but a compounding wealth of ever more refined relationships between the person and increasingly differentiated parts of the rest of the world. Searles is emphatic that "world" means the nonhuman as well as the human, not only as the object of the linkages, but as the means and symbols of them.

The culmination of this refined difference-with-affinity is a firm ground of personal confidence and membership in its largest sense. And here I may rub the modern philosopher the wrong way, for I see in Carleton Coon's *The Hunting Peoples* the best description of that peculiar blend of loyalty and tolerance spanning the gap between separateness and belonging, forming a tapestry of ideas, feelings, speculation, experiences, and body that is Me, related to the multitude out there, from human brothers to the distant stars, that are the Other. Given this foundation and some intelligence, the years of tribal experience may produce wisdom, the most mature expression of which is the capacity to gently bring others forward to it, as far as they are capable.

Finally, that ethos of small-group tribal counsel with its advisory leadership, hospitality, and tolerance toward outsiders, perception of nature as a sacred language, and the quality of mentorship by which the young are coached was understood and exemplified by John Collier (d. 1968). His compassion for the American Indians was compounded by his knowledge of the caliber of those societies the whites had destroyed. In his eighty years he grew in sweetness and in tender understanding of his adversaries as well as his supporters both within and without tribal America. In age, he himself showed where the foundations of the first twenty years can lead. I think his maturity was most clearly manifest in his conviction of the goodness of creation and in his sense of being at home in the world.

The adult in full realization of his potential both uses and experiences the non-human world in characteristic ways, particularly in approaching it as both instrument and counterplayer, gift and home, and particularly not as an escape from or alternative to interpersonal and social relationships. To be fully mature, as Rollo May says, is to understand and to affirm limitations. There is also inherent in maturity an acceptance of ambiguity, of the tensions between the lust for omnipotence and the necessity to manipulate, between man as different and man as a kind of animal, and especially between a growing sense of the separateness of the self and kinship to the Other, achieved through an ever-deepening fullness of personal identity, defined by a web of relationship and metaphorical common ground. Harold Searles' remark is to the point: "It seems to me that the *highest* order of maturity is essential to the achievement of a reality relatedness with that which is *most unlike* oneself." Maturity emerges in midlife as the result of the demands of an innate calendar of growth phases, to which the human nurturers—parents, friends, teachers—have responded in season. It celebrates a central analogy of self and world in ever-widening spheres of meaning and participation, not an ever-growing domination over nature, escape in abstractions, or existential funk.

The human, twenty-year psychogenesis evolved because it was adaptive and beneficial to survival; its phases were specialized, integral to individual growth in the physical and cultural environments of the emergence of our species. And there is the rub—in those environments: small-group, leisured, foraging life-ways with natural surroundings.[2] For us, now, that world no longer exists. The culmination of individual ontogenesis, characterized by graciousness, tolerance, and forbearance, tradition-bound to accommodate a mostly nonhuman world, and given to long, indulgent training of the young, may be inconsistent in some ways with the needs of society. In such societies—and I include ours—certain infantile qualities might work better: fear of separation, fantasies of omnipotence, oral preoccupation, tremors of helplessness, and bodily incompetence and dependence. Biological evolution is not involved, as it works much too slowly to make adjustments in our species in these ten millennia since the archaic foraging cultures began to be destroyed by their hostile, aggressive, better-organized, civilized neighbors. Programmed for the slow development toward a special kind of sagacity, we live in a world where that humility and tender sense of human limitation is no longer rewarded. Yet we suffer for the want of that vanished world, a deep grief we learn to misconstrue.

In the civilized world the roles of authority—family heads and others in power—were filled increasingly with individuals in a sense incomplete, who would in turn select and coach underlings flawed like themselves. Perhaps no one would be aware of such a trend, which would advance by pragmatic success across the generations as society put its fingers gropingly on the right moments in child nurturing by taking mothers off to work, spreading their attention and energy too thin with a houseful of babies, altering games and stories, manipulating anxiety in the child in a hundred possible ways. The transitory and normally healthful features of adolescence—narcissism, oedipal fears and loyalties, ambivalence and inconstancy, playing with words, the gang connection—might in time be honored in patriotic idiom and philosophical axiom. The primary impulses of infancy can be made to seem essential to belief, to moral superiority, masked by the psychological defenses of repression and projection. Over the centuries major institutions and metaphysics might finally celebrate attitudes and ideas originating in the normal context of immaturity, the speculative throes of adolescence, the Freudian psychosexual phases, or in even earlier neonatal or prenatal states.

Probably such ontogenetic crippling carries with it into adult life some traits that no society wants, but gets because they are coupled in some way with the childish will to destroy and other useful regressions, fellow travelers with ugly effects. Perhaps there is no way to perpetuate a suckling's symbiosis with mother as a religious ideal without dragging up painful unconscious memories of an inadequate body boundary or squeamishness about being cut loose.

In our time, youthfulness is a trite ideal, but even in those peasant and village societies where youth is "kept in its place," the traces of immaturity in cultural themes invite our scrutiny. That European medieval children were said to have no childhood as we understand it is suggestive of the omissions and constrictions that serve this socially adaptive crippling.

The person himself is, of course, caught between his inner calendar and the surgeries of society. His momentum for further growth may be twisted or amputated according to the hostilities, fears, or fantasies required of him, as his retardation is silently engineered to domesticate his integrity or to allow him to share in the collective dream of mastery.

I have chosen, arbitrarily, four historical periods in which to examine the mutilations of personal maturity as the vehicle of cultural progress and environmental decimation. They seem to offer especially good possibilities for seeking the impact of this process on the relation of man to nature. These are the earliest agriculture, the era of the desert fathers, the Reformation, and present-day industrial society. They are merely focal points in what may have been a continuing dedevelopment, but I submit that they first began with a slight twist in the life of the child, with events that may only have marred his capacity for elderhood and judgment. If so, the history of Western man has been a progressive peeling back of the psyche, as if the earliest agriculture may have addressed itself to extenuation of adolescent concerns while the most modern era seeks to evoke in society at large some of the fixations of early natality—rationalized, symbolized, and disguised as need be. The individual growth curve, as described by Bruno Bettelheim, Jean Piaget, Erik Erikson, and others, is a biological heritage of the deep past. It is everyman's tree of life, now pruned by civic gardeners as the outer branches and twigs become incompatible with the landscaped order.

The reader may extend that metaphor as he wishes, but I shall move to an animal image to suggest that the only society more frightful than one run by children, as in Golding's *Lord of the Flies,* might be one run by childish adults.

2

The Domesticators

Of HALF THE TIME since the beginning of the momentous revolution by which agriculture and village life began to reshape the condition of human existence we know almost nothing of the *felt experience*. On how the world was seen we have only surmises based on bits of material culture, dug up like fossil imprints of ideas. Archaeology tells us that the first crops preceded the making of cities by about five thousand years. The fifty centuries from here back to that point of earliest urbanity, to the wheel and the advent of writing, embracing the whole tumult of civilized man, were prepared for and made possible by the quiet fifty centuries before that.

Few prehistorians suppose that those earliest farmers and first domesticators east of the Mediterranean Sea were conscious revolutionaries or even that changes were dramatic in a single lifetime.[1] In many ways, life was modified gradually from that of their hunter-gatherer ancestors, whose modest relics in turn stretch back three million years to the beginning of the Pleistocene. Yet, by the time civilization began in the great city-states of Egypt and Mesopotamia, the tradesmen, bureaucrats, and tillers of the soil exceeded their hunter forebears in possessions, and altered their surroundings—and were the creators and victims of new attitudes, expectations, and mythology. How that transition toward urbanism took place we may guess only with educated uncertainty.

A different style of consciousness among the ancestors of Western tradition in the savannas, grasslands, and forest margins of what are now Egypt, Turkey, Iraq, Jordan, Iran, Syria, Lebanon, Israel, and Russia between the Black and Caspian seas characterizes the psychohistory of the emergence of sedentary village life from nomadic foraging. It was not simply a matter of being outdoors or being in. The archaic hunters were indoors when they occupied rock shelters or built houses, while some of the earliest food collectors and goat keepers, on the other hand, lived in caves and, like the hunters, spent seasons in the open. Foraging and gathering graded into collecting, planting, cultivating, and trading. The farmer and herder never ceased to do some hunting. The steps from gathering wild fruits to gathering-planting the seeds of the ancestral barley and wheat, from hunting to driving-hunting the wild ancestors of the goat and sheep, from the scavenging wolf-dog ancestor to the dog/man collaboration cover a long period of transition and overlap. Even after village life was established on a year-round basis and the seven- or eight-score inhabitants were dependent on plant crops and domesticated animals, artifacts of stone continued to be made. Pottery, weaving—the paraphernalia we normally associate with agriculture and village life—came bit by bit, here and there, in some places disappeared and came again.

Changes in thought, perceptions of the outer and inner world, and premises and assumptions about reality probably occurred in a similar capricious, spasmodic way, themes formulated and voiced and ritually assimilated only to be lost and then rearticulated. It was a long period of tenuous concepts, intimations, oblique views of older wisdom, shifts in perspective toward concepts of the world that, by the time of the Egyptian dynasties or Mesopotamian civilizations would be extremely different from those of the Paleolithic past. These shifts have to do with the *quality of attention* rather than ideas; with the *significance of place* rather than the identity of nations; with the theme of *duality;* with the subtle effects of food and *trophic patterns* on thought and expression; with the accumulation of made things and *possessions* that was part of village life; and, finally, with some of the subtler influences of *domestication* on the ways people saw themselves and the land, as well as their plants and animals.

Quality of attention means cultural and habitual differences in the style of day-to-day hearing, seeing, smelling, tasting, and touching the surroundings. These differences are perhaps not as striking in times of crisis or formal expression as in the more casual way in which we pay heed. What people notice, what they expect to encounter, the mix of senses used, even the quality of their inattention and disregard all reveal something about the kind of world it is for them.

These early farming villagers were probably much like their hunter forebears in their vigilant sensitivity to sound. Walter J. Ong speaks of this sensitivity as an orientation to interiority. All sound is a voice—dynamic, revealing, and communicating. Even today such an attitude of listening is apparent among peasants or shepherds for whom the farmstead or flock is a dynamic mosaic in their care, sometimes not all visible from minute to minute. The cacophony with which the still-larger town would eventually bullyrag and deaden the ear was yet to be, although perhaps its first signs could be noticed in the differences between that vast and articulate silence surrounding men in wild landscapes and the soft babble of the rural village that blocked off the voices of the distant savanna and forest—in the daytime at least. In the village few sounds were surprising, and most were fixed in place, like the familiar scratch of a broom on a known doorstep at a regular time.

Attention to visual cues even more clearly differentiates

the hunter from the villager. "The hunter," says Ortega y Gasset, "does not look tranquilly in one determined direction, sure beforehand that the game will pass in front of him. The hunter knows that he does not know what is going to happen . . . thus he needs to prepare an attention which does not consist in riveting itself on the presumed but consists precisely in not presuming anything and in avoiding innattentiveness. It is a 'universal' attention, which does not inscribe itself on any point and tries to be on all points."[2] For the most part the animals—or roots, berries, and nuts—the hunter-gatherer seeks are unseen and hidden. In this sense his gathering, though directed to plants fixed in place, is unlike the farmer's harvest. Although wild plants and animals have their seasonal and habitat tendencies, any one kind of dozens might be encountered, and the signs that indicate their whereabouts are myriad. As the food collector became the planter, much of that awareness of a moving or hidden object was exchanged for a different kind of mystery—that of generation itself—which invited the focused imagination at the expense of keenness of looking and listening.

The plants used by these earliest farmers were increasingly annual grasses; most of the garden vegetables that would eventually join them were annuals too. As planters they were thereby attuned to the weather and calendar, an awareness that would become meteorology and astronomy. Their hunting ancestors were sensitive to these things but were not faced with the same potential calamities of weather, for their more varied diet and the longer cycle of animal growth and perennial plant foods blunted bad years. The change to the cultivation of annuals was critical in the reshaping of attention, for the seasonal pattern of the birth, growth, death, and rebirth of the crops would burn itself into the minds of these grain farmers so profoundly that it might be said to be the first feature—the kernel even—of civilized thought. If these farmers ceased to listen to a million secret tongues in the wilderness it was, in retrospect, to develop techniques of domestication with which to alter the earth and to gain a symbolic foundation for a vision of a cyclic cosmology and eventually a concept of immortality.

I do not want to overstate the narrowing effect of season and climate on the farmer. The hunter's attitude of avoiding inattentiveness persisted in the farmer's style inasmuch as hunting and gathering persisted, especially in the earlier centuries of agriculture. And, of course, the march of the seasons, which to our eyes seems coarse, is to practiced observers subject to the most delicate nuances, such as the schedule of flowering of wild plants, the breeding cycle of birds, and the emergence and behavior of insects. This phenology of emergence and metamorphosis has a daily and hourly character throughout the year, to which I suspect the early domesticators were, like good naturalists, as sensitive as their foraging cousins.[3] Perhaps the first subtle warpings of this consciousness were matters of emphasis, shaped as much by the diminished variety of wild things at hand in the village vicinity as by the needs of their domestic plantings.

A village alters the relative abundance of wild and tame creatures that are in concentric zones around it. Each such human community of domestication had its own history, its own relationship to terrain, water supplies, fuel, building materials, and so on that modified the general pattern of clustered dwellings and gradated intensities of use away from the center. The village and its landscape became a place physically as well as psychologically unlike the camps and transient shelters that men had made in earlier times.

The *significance of place* to such peoples as Australian aborigines can be very different from its significance to sedentary peoples—certainly far more profound than simple location.

Individual and tribal identity are built up in connection with widely separate places and the paths connecting them. Different places are successively assimilated or internalized. They become distinct, though unconscious, elements of the self, enhanced by mythology and ceremony, generating a network of deep emotional attachments that cements the personality. Throughout life, those places have a role in the evocation of self and group consciousness. They are mnemonic: integrated components of a sacred history and the remembered and unconsciously felt past. The whole of the known region or home range becomes a hierophantic map, a repository of the first creation that parallels and overlies individual history. Something like this is known to be typical of many nonliterate peoples and was probably true of prehistoric peoples as well.[4] Juvenile imprinting on terrain (that is, indelible fixation on specific sites, giving them lifetime supersignificance) continues among modern urban people as well, so it is not unlikely that some form of dynamic integration of the identity formation of the individual with features of the terrain is part of human biology, a genetic heritage; but the mode by which sedentary peoples would employ the landscape psychodynamically, as a tool of self-recognition, is quite different from that of the hunter.

The hunter was mobile, like his prey, the big-game animals. The topographic features and creatures were diffused throughout a vast region. They were not all visible at once and human products were always mixed with the nonhuman. The villager did not rove through these physical extensions of the self; he occupied them. The hunter seemed to inhabit the land body like a blood corpuscle, while the farmer was centered in it and could scan it as a whole.

As villages grew and their populations increased, they became more territorial—embedded, so to speak, in a defended location. Hunter-foragers before them (as today among the

relict tribes of Australia) had often a jealous sense of occupancy and strict mores respecting trespass, but the matter was
settled in formalities and protocol. It became far more feasi-
ble for five hundred men to exclude outsiders from fifteen
square miles than it had been for ten to bar interlopers from
fifteen hundred square miles. Perhaps what is known today as
"body-boundary phenomena"—the totality of feelings which
constitute the private sense of one's own shape and surface
—became more rigid and shell-like where the metaphors of
self, tribe, and place became more tightly structured, the various levels of boundary reinforcing each other.[5]

Among villagers, the limits of territorial lands were
marked by stones identified with protective spirits.[6] These
boundaries often ran along watershed divides and were therefore in the highest places. The fertile lowland, circumscribed
at the horizon and protected there by sacred pillars, may be
seen as analogous to a gigantic body. Its contours, springs,
caves, vegetation, and landforms are the surface of a giant,
like a sheltering and nourishing mother. The concept of the
Great Mother Earth is, in this way, a natural metaphor for
sedentary peoples. So it became, for agricultural peoples, the
dominant mythological figure.

The maternal image had not been celebrated so single-
mindedly among their hunter predecessors. Although carv-
ings that may represent pregnant women are known from the
Pleistocene hunting cultures of Europe, there is no evidence
as to how they were used or whether they indeed referred to
motherhood rather than matehood; and there is little else
from the Stone Age to suggest the concept of the Great
Mother.[7]

But this concept was highly developed, in one form or
another, in all the great agricultural civilizations of the preclassical Western world, a psychological reference point as
well as a religious symbol. It shows a shift in the iconography

of farmers, a focusing on the nourishing and protective aspects of the world, evoking the experience of being mothered. The gods were becoming more humanlike, the plants and animals subordinated to a kind of family drama. The world of the imagination, as well as the tangible surroundings, was in this way saturated with human bodies and faces, emphasizing personality and gender. The animals did not simply give way to humans in these symbolic roles, but were subordinated in cosmology to manlike gods in a new and more presumptuous way.[8]

To the hunter, much of what he had seemed given; to the farmer, earned by continuing labor. For the farmer the contrast between the ease of childhood and the burdens of maturity had increased. For him there was a lost, more perfect world, the images of which were enhanced by his awareness of this contrast.[9] Mircea Eliade tells us that the myth of that loss is as wide as humanity, but the question must remain— for it has not been addressed directly by him—as to the difference in its meaning to farmers and their nonfarming ancestors. Surely the biblical Garden of Eden story must have seemed perverse to those hunting peoples on whom missionaries inflicted it (but whose courtesy and good humor compelled them to stifle their laughter). That myth has the fully developed features of a consumate agricultural dream: no work, bad weather, or wild beasts; no dependents, competitors, risk, curiosity, old age, alienation from God, death, or women's troubles—not that some of these ideals would not have occurred to hunters. What its collective form was among early planters we cannot know, but we can suspect this much: the crops must now and again have failed, plunging the individual into torments of anxiety reminiscent of those earlier "failings" of their own mothers. Over the centuries, soils and productivity declined, were eroded away, or salted in, requiring more work for a meager subsistence. Alternative foods in the wild lands were extirpated. Drought and parasites found the worn community more vulnerable. The inevitable decline from original productivity and stability was known by tradition and carried with it a sense of grievous loss and punishment. In the decline of its former radiance, the earth seemed to be sullied, and the fault or guilt to lie with man himself.[10]

While the farmer would eventually come to see himself at odds with the wandering hunters and pastoralists and would resent their freedom as shiftlessness and the relative ease of their lives as sloth, these earliest farmers were still part-time hunters. "Eden was no garden," writes Nigel Calder, but it was a gathering paradise.[11]

In any case, the Earth Mother herself would come in for some suspicion in the same spirit in which Eve would be blamed. The bad Mother Earth—as well as the good—was implicit in the attribution of gender to the soil, for there is a time in infancy when the mother is indeed two persons, one of whom is fearfully and infuriatingly withholding.[12] I suppose that men who till the earth everywhere have in some fashion experienced and codified the environment as parental, although their particular social and kinship systems both evoke and represent the parental cosmos in unique local ways. How out of blood and marriage ties the different kinship patterns arose, the anthropologists have not yet fully explained, though it is a fair guess that there are consistent differences between hunters and farmers and between grain farmers and root farmers.[13] If so, attitudes toward the feminine earth may be influenced by the role of women in a particular society and the land used accordingly—land use and mother use mutually interacting. Also, the mother is very different to the small infant than to the child and different again to the pubertal youth, so that a whole series of different "mothers" are accumulated during the growth of each individual. A culture may foster certain of these in its symbolic life and neglect others. External nature may become part of the language as well as the object of such portraits.

Crippling as the image may be of the land as a fecund goddess—even as the basis of a supposed matriarchate in Crete and Anatolia—we should perhaps reserve judgment as to its ecological efficacy. The metaphor of the great goddess enables emotions and bonds of kinship, compassion, and responsibility to be felt not only within the human group but to be directed to the earth, helping the group to survive in health the experience of the ecological double-bind: the fertile earth that sometimes fails to produce.

The negative effects are obscured by the forces of repression. What are the results of a lifelong subordination to mother? Among them are resentment and masked retaliations, displaced acts of violence, and the consequent guilt— all of which can be exploited to intensify the maternal dependence. Here I wish only to raise the question whether lifelong subordination to a vast Earth Mother might not affect men in similar ways.

In many ways the sensory impact of village life fostered an impression of opposition, or *duality:* things were in or of the community and village or they were not, they favored the crops or hindered them, were wild or tame, weeds or crops, useful or worthless. The same thunderstorm that could have multiple and diverse effects on the hunter's life because of the variety of his interests and foods was plainly destructive or quenching to the village whose garden and drinking water would suffer drought or flood of increasing severity as the natural vegetation and soil diminished.

In the simplified ecosystem of agriculture it would be possible to adopt, as it were, the posture of jural duality that enables the juvenile, newly caught up in the spirit of his burgeoning sense of ethics, to make judgments with overweening certainty.[14]

The simplified world of the ancient dry-land farmer was,

in spite of its clarity, not necessarily a more coherent one than that of his ancestors. Its ambivalence was not in its multiplicity, but in the inherent conflict of things in opposition. Instead of a peacefully integrating dusk, the night swept away the light of day like a cavalry charge. Dryness and wetness struggled for the land. The hunters, says Eliade, tended to face up to these ambiguities and to reconcile them in their mythology, while the farmers, among whom they were perhaps more tragically crucial, repressed them.[15]

The resolution of such seeming contradictions is a mark of mature thought and personality. For the small child, a kind of bimodality of cognition is normal, a part of the beginnings of classifying and making categories, an essential step in the adult capacity to make abstractions. The world at first is an either/or place. The human mind makes a hazardous trip, beginning in an undivided unity—the I-am-everything paradise of the fetus—proceeding through a world of contrarities, and arriving at maturity able to work in multiplicity and plurality. Getting stuck in the binary view strands the adult in a universe torn by a myriad of oppositions and conflicts.

But this kind of splitting remained to be fully realized in the patriarchal societies. For the planters the reconciliation was symbolized by the figure of the earth as a woman and her marriage to a son who must die, the virgin mother-wife and murdered son-king. Such a mother is the unconscious ideal of preadolescent boys, whose spontaneous affection for their mothers is never completely lost, nor in some important ways surpassed by love of wife. The "death" of their childhood does not catapult them into a totally masculinist world as it does among patriarchal peoples, but only foreshadows a new birth in a "uterine" relationship with a larger mother.

The psychology of this celestial round—life cycle and crop cycle—is one of regression rather than growth. This mother worship on a cosmic scale is achieved by exaggeration of that preadolescent state, formalized in the endless round by the ritual supplication and courtship of the Great Mother Earth. It centers on a fantasy that perpetuates a defense against oedipal tension and blocks its resolution and the mature possibilities that follow.

Hunters were certainly aware of the cycle of annual renewal, but the early farmers had reason to be more intent on the metaphors of seed germination and the estrus of cattle. Much of the ancient art now in museums reveals an obsession with the great round of the year, perhaps because of the increasing uncertainty of yield and because the farmer had fewer alternatives than his foraging ancestors. With agriculture it was likely to be boom or bust, and in the bad years nature seemed to withhold that to which the farmer, after all his labor, felt he had a right.

There can arise, says Harold Searles, "a transference to all of outer reality as personifying, in unconscious experience, a dominating, withholding mother."[16] In effect, the child of a mother who *seems* to be malevolently deficient—or, for that matter, absent—can begin to see the whole world through the same lenses of projection and recrimination.

The figure of the great mother goddess is central to the food or *trophic pattern* that governs domestic life. After nearly ten thousand years of living with that apprehension about food and the binding force of its psychic disablement, it is not surprising that civilized people find it difficult to understand the absence of such worries among hunting-gathering peoples, making them seem careless and imprudent.[17] The repressed distrust of the mother and the maternal earth can then be redirected onto those blithe savages, picturing them as unfeeling for the well-being of their families and coarsely inured to hunger and the other imagined afflictions of a brutish life. This scornful fantasy is easily enough projected upon the rest of brute creation, making it easier to believe that all animals are insentient.

It is not only an abstract Mother Earth who is the victim of this psychic deformity, but all wild things. Characteristically, farmers and townsmen do not study and speculate on wild animals or "think" them in their poetic mystery and complex behaviors. With civilization, typically fewer than twenty kinds of plants and animals in one village were tended, herded, sheltered, planted, cultivated, fertilized, harvested, cured, stored, and distributed. Sacrifice and other ceremonial activity were restricted accordingly. Even the gradual broadening of agriculture to embrace many more kinds of organisms left it far short of the rich cosmos of the hunter. Civilization increased the separation between the individual and the natural world as it did the child from the mother, amplifying an attachment that could be channeled into aggression.

The farmer and his village brethren assumed an executive task of food production, storage, and distribution that would weigh heavily on them for the same reason that all executives wear out their nerves and glands: responsibility in a situation of certain failure—if not this year, then next, or the year after that. Being held responsible for things beyond their control is especially crushing for children, for whom the world may become hopelessly chaotic.[18] They, in their chores of goat tending or other work tasks, like the adults who managed the domesticated community, were vulnerable to weather, marauders, pests, and the demons of earth and air. Blights and witherings were inevitable, bringing not only food shortage but emotional onslaughts. The judgment is guilt, for which the penalty is scarcity.

In such a world the full belly is never enough. Like the dour Yankee farmer who sees in the clear blue sky of a Vermont spring day "a damned weather-breeder," abundance would only set the mark by which shortage would be measured.

But quantity was not the only variable. As the diversity of foods diminished—the wild alternatives becoming scarcer and more distant from villages—the danger of malnutrition increased. It is widely observed that domesticated varieties of fruits and vegetables differ from their wild ancestors in carbohydrate/protein/fat ratios as well as vitamin and mineral content. Where selection is for appearance, size, storability, or even taste, some food value may be lost. Virtually all the processes that aid storage or preservation have a similar price in decline of quality. The point is that the lack of food is not the only spur to a kind of trophic obsession, but the hungers of those who are superficially well fed might also add to this general picture of chronic preoccupation with food.

The argument can be made that anything that fixates the individual's attention on food can be associated with ontogenetic regression. I mean not only the infantile impatience to eat and the whole alimentary oral-anal romance to which he is so responsive, but the typical conservatism of older children and adolescents—the first, perhaps because of a sensitivity to strong or strange new flavors; the second, because of a psychic state in which the groping for a new selfhood is partly one of recognition of codes that identify a group. Teenagers are the weakest gourmets because they have not yet achieved a confident-enough identity to free themselves to develop personal preferences. The young are wary about what they eat, probably for adaptive as well as culturally functional reasons.

The young of hunter societies are probably cautious too, and certainly such cultures had a highly developed sense of food taboos. Nonetheless, the small foraging band ate dozens of kinds of flesh (including invertebrates) and scores of kinds of roots, nuts, vegetables, and leaves. The idea that this range was born of desperation is not supported by the evidence. There were certainly seasonal opportunities and choices, but apparently to be human is to be omnivorous, to show an open, experimental attitude toward what is edible, guided by an educated taste and a wide range of options. As among all peoples, what is eaten or not eaten had cultural limits among hunter-foragers, but these did not prevent somebody in a group from eating at least some parts of almost anything.[19]

The food-producing societies that succeeded the hunter-gatherers attempted to make virtue of defect by intensifying the cultural proscriptions on what was to be eaten in a world where, for most people, there were fewer choices than their archaic ancestors enjoyed. And how was this tightening of the belt and expanded contempt achieved? It was built into the older child and adolescent. It could be frozen at that level as part of a more general developmental check. It may have been inevitable in the shift from totemic to caste thought about animals, corresponding to the change from hunting to farming, in which wild animals ceased to be used as metaphors central to personal identity, to be less involved with analogies of assimilation and incorporation. The growth of self-identity requires coming to terms with the wild and uncontrollable within. Normally the child identifies frightening feelings and ideas with specific external objects. The sensed limitations of such objects aid his attempts to control his fears. As the natural containers for these projected feelings receded with the wilderness, a lack of substitutes may have left the child less able to cope and thus more dependent, his development impaired.

Perhaps there was no more dramatic change in the transition from hunting-gathering to farming than in the kind and number of *possessions*. Among archaic people who use no beasts of burden, true possessions are few and small. What objects are owned are divided between those privately held and those in which there is a joint interest. Among the latter, such as religious objects or the carcass of a game animal, the individual shares obligations as well as benefits, but in neither case does he accumulate or seem to feel impoverished. The wariness of gifts and the lack of accumulation found in these people are not due to nomadism, for the desire would still be evident.[20] Nor can these characteristics be explained away as a culturally conditioned materialism, as that would beg the question.

This absence of wanting belongings seems more likely to be part of a psychological dimension of human life and its modification in civilization. "Belongings" is an interesting word, referring to membership and therefore to parts of a whole. If that whole is Me, then perhaps the acquisition of mostly man-made objects can contribute in some way to my identity—a way that may compensate for some earlier means lost when people became sedentary and their world mostly man-made landscapes. Or, if objects fail to fully suffice, we want more and more, as we crave more of a pain-killing drug. In short, what is it about the domesticated civilized world that alters the concept of self so that it is enhanced by property?

My self is to some extent made by me, at least insofar as I seem to gain control over it. A wilderness environment is, on the contrary, mostly given. For the hunter-forager, this Me in a non-Me world is the most penetrating and powerful realization in life. The mature person in such a culture is not concerned with blunting that dreadful reality but with establishing lines of connectedness or relationship. Formal culture is shaped by the elaboration of covenants and negotiations with the Other. The separation makes impossible a fuzzy confusion; there is no vague "identity with nature," but rather a lifelong task of formulating—and internalizing—treaties of affiliation. The forms and terms of that relationship become part of a secondary level of my identity, the background or gestalt. This refining of what-I-am-not is a developmental matter, and the human life cycle conforms to stages in its progress.

Now consider the process in a world in which that Other has mostly disappeared. Food, tools, animals, structures, whole landscapes are man-made; even to me personally they seem more made than given and serve as extensions of that part of the self which I determine. My infantile ego glories in this great consuming I-am. Everything in sight belongs to me in the same sense as my members: legs, arms, hands, and so on. The buildings, streets, and cultivated fields are all continuous with my voluntary nervous system, my tamed, controlled self.

In the ideology of farming, wild things are enemies of the tame; the wild Other is not the context but the opponent of "my" domain. Impulses, fears, and dreams—the realm of the unconscious—no longer are represented by the community of wild things with which I can work out a meaningful relationship. The unconscious is driven deeper and away with the wilderness. New definitions of the self by trade and political subordination in part replace the metaphoric reciprocity between natural and cultural in the totemic life of the hunter-foragers. But the new system defines by exclusion. What had been a complementary entity embracing friendly and dangerous parts in a unified cosmos now takes on the colors of hostility and fragmentation. Even where the great earth religions of high agriculture tend to mend this rupture in the mythology of the symbolic mother, its stunting of the identity process remains.

Although he formulated the cognitive distinctions between totemic culture, with its analogy of a system of differences in nonhuman nature as a paradigm for the organization of culture, and caste or agriculture, which find models for

35

human relationships in the types of things made, Levi-Strauss avoided the psychological developmental implications with admirable caution. But it is clear from the developmental scheme of Erikson that fine mastery of the neuromuscular system, self-discipline of the body, the emergence of skills, and awakening to tools are late-juvenile and early-adolescent concerns. In farming, the land itself becomes a tool, an instrument of production, a possession that is at once the object and implement of vocation as well as a definer of the self.

As farming shifts from subsistence to monoculture, village specialists who do not themselves cultivate the soil appear. Their roles are psychologically and mythically reintegrated into society as a whole. Smith, potter, clerk, and priest become constituents of the new reality. That reality is for them all like the pot to the potter:

(1) the wild world has reduced significance in his own conscious identity and may therefore be perceived (along with some part of himself) as chaotic; (2) he himself, like his pot, is a static *made* object, and, by inference, so is the rest of society and the world; (3) there is a central core of nonlivingness in himself; (4) the ultimate refinements in his unique self are to be achieved by acts of will or creativity; (5) daily labor —routine, repetitive motions for long hours at a time—is at the heart of his being; (6) his relationship to others is based on an exchange of possessions, and the accumulation of them is a measure of his personal achievement; and (7) the nonhuman world is primarily a source of substance to be shaped or made by man, as it was mythically by God.

These are but fragments of the world of the artisan. Gradations exist between that world and totemic cultures. The transition took many centuries before man's concept of the wilderness was indeed defined by the first synonym in Roget's *Thesaurus:* "disorder." In the earliest farming societies perhaps there were only nuances of the psychology of domestication. The individual would not see himself as a possession or conceive of being possessed by others until tribal villages coalesced into chiefdoms and he was conscripted or enslaved or his labor sold as a commodity, events that may have been as much an outcome as a cause of the new consciousness. That was many generations in the future as the first harvesters of wild wheat began to save some grains to plant. Yet we see them headed, however tentatively, toward the view of the planet as a thing rather than a thou, a product instead of an organism, to be possessed rather than encountered as a presence.

This attitude connects with the psychological position of early infancy, when differentiation between the living and the nonliving is still unclear. The badly nurtured infant may become imprinted with the hardness of its cradle or bottle so irreversibly that it cannot, even as an adult, form fully caring human relationships. But that is the extreme case. The earliest farmers were inclined to represent the landscape as a living being, even, at first, to conceive life in made things. But as those things became commodities and infancy was reshaped accordingly, the cosmos would become increasingly ambiguous. Attempts to resolve this conflict between the "it-ness" and the numen of things—both in the landscape and its reciprocal, the inner self—are a major goal of the religious and cultural activity of civilization.[21]

The *domestication* of animals had effects on human perception that went far beyond its economic implications. Men had been observing animals closely as a major intellectual activity for several million years. They have not been deterred, even by so momentous a change in the condition of man/animal relationship as domestication, but the message has been altered. Changes in the animals themselves, brought about by captivity and breeding programs, are widely recognized.

These changes include plumper and more rounded features, greater docility and submissiveness, reduced mobility, simplification of complex behaviors (such as courtship), the broadening or generalizing of signals to which social responses are given (such as following behavior), reduced hardiness, and less specialized environmental and nutritional requirements. The sum effect of these is infantilization.[22] The new message is an emotional appeal, sense of mastery, and relative simplicity of animal life. The style conveyed as a metaphor by the wild animal is altered to literal model and metonymic subordinate: life is inevitable physical deformity and limitation, mindless frolic and alarms, bluntness, following and being herded, being fertile when called upon, representing nature at a new, cruder level.

One or another of the domesticated forms was widely used as a substitute in human relations: as slave, sexual partner, companion, caretaker, family member. Animal and human discriminations that sustained barriers between species were breached, suggesting nothing so much in human experience as the very small child's inability to see the difference between dogs and cows. Pet-keeping, virtually a civilized institution, is an abyss of covert and unconscious uses of animals in the service of psychological needs, glossed over as play and companionship.[23] The more extremely perverted private abuse of animals grades off into the sadistic slaughter of animals in public spectacles, of which the modern bullfight is an extravagant example.

Before civilization, animals were seen as belonging to their own nation and to be the bearers of messages and gifts of meat from a sacred domain. In the village they became possessions. Yet ancient avatars, they remained fascinating in human eyes. A select and altered little group of animals, filtered through the bottleneck of domestication, came in human experience to represent the whole of animals of value to people. The ancient human approach to consciousness by seeing—or discovering—the self through other eyes and the need to encounter the otherness of the cosmos in its kindred aspect were two of the burdens thrust upon these deformed creatures. To educate his powers of discrimination and wonder, the child, born to expect subtle and infinite possibilities, was presented with fat hulks, vicious manics, and hypertrophied drudges. The psychological introjection of these as part of the self put the child on a detour in the developmental process that would culminate in a dead end, posted "You can't get there from here."

These six aspects of civilized thought originating in agriculture—quality of attention, significance of place, duality, trophic anxiety, attitude toward possessions, and domestication—are not so much characteristics as trends. After all, some wild things survived even in dooryards, and human foraging continues. But the combined effect of all the changes in plant-animal abundance, including replacement of a multitude of wild forms in the village surround by a small number of domestic forms, was the creation of a new kind of landscape, itself made more immature. Ecologically, husbandry destroys the mature ecosystem or climax community. In its place there appear assemblages of plants and animals typical of earlier stages. Ecologist Eugene Odum speaks of the whole series as a developmental sequence, analogous to that of human growth. Generally, the earlier phases are simpler, less efficient, and less stable than the later, but, if left to themselves, go through a predictable species replacement until, after many years, that replacement tends to diminish and the community has regained its climax, its primeval or virgin condition.[24]

The husbandman, however, does not want his meadows to get brushy or his gardens to get weedy. By keeping stock in

39

the meadow, he stabilizes its altered, youthful state; its continued stabilization results in a plateau of unaltered immaturity, a disclimax. The disclimaxes that appeared with the first farming in the foothills of the Near East, like all subsequent disclimaxes, seem thematically harmonious with the ambience of immaturity of human thought and the human community proper. In an essay in 1942, Ortega y Gasset speaks of the mature climax ecosystem as "authentic countryside." He writes, "Only the hunting ground is true countryside . . . neither farmland, nor battleground, nor tourist country." Only there, in the "first countryside, the only 'natural' one, can we succeed in emigrating from our human world to an authentic 'outside,' from which history represents the retreat or anabasis."[25] Mindful of the achievements of history, it is nonetheless this chance to get outside oneself that concerns us here, for it is needed repeatedly, in different stages of individual development, and in different forms. Ortega y Gasset's countryside and Odum's climax community are common ground. They are for the older child and adolescent a penultimate encounter at the end of a sequence of experiences of otherness that began with the awareness of mother as a separate being.

In the foregoing pages I have suggested a number of ways in which tending crops and village life made problems for the farmer that were psychologically similar to and in tandem with typical difficulties of the early growth of the individual. Each of them in some way seemed to increase the physical and perceptual distance between the person and those forms of the nonhuman world most remote from him. By aggravating the tensions of separation from the mother and at the same time spatially isolating the individual from the nonhumanized world, agriculture made it difficult for the developing person to approach the issues around which the crucial passages into fully mature adult life had been structured in the course of human existence.

New beginnings are always in some sense regressive. The farmer, caught in the net of the seasons, is a victim of his own earth metaphors. His ceremonial life, expressively formulated in homologies of the self and the cosmos, invades the whole of his annual round with avatars of germination, fruition, and early death. His horizons become more limited in space as well as time, suggestive of the homebody tenor and prepubertal fears of wandering too far. His restricted geography is like a hobble on his distancing from the womb, contrasted with those tests and trials by which his forefathers measured the maturity of the individual by sending him alone into wild countryside and solitude.

Everything worked to bind the new farmer to locality, to encourage the vision of the land as part of himself and to dream of a better world, of a lost unity—with its silent evocation of his unconscious memory of the natal state. Even when the mother figure was extended to the land, it reflected a symbiosis more akin to the infant's love/hate for her than to the interrelated but independent species in an ecosystem. Matriarchy as a political system may never have existed, but the exercise of male power was, in the end, to master those processes that would produce and reproduce for him, even while the final maternal secrets were out of his reach. Male sway would gain him possessions, too, which the ancient hunters had known would not ensure either a true self, or, in the last analysis, respect; to give away what they had was the lesson they had learned. It was not that the villager *would not* learn that lesson, but that he *could not.* His identity was spread around among things, insufficiently internalized and consolidated. Foremost among them were the products of his labor. The classes of made objects seem, almost as though by some mysterious dynamic, to have superseded totemic membership as the touchstone of those episodes of initiation by which the adult learns who he is. With the made thing at the center of his being, the villager felt that he himself was made, and he would, thereafter, see the world that way too.

He came to live more and more with his own fabrications as the environment. Being of his own making, the things around him were indistinct from himself, and he was less differentiated than he wanted to be. At such a level of psychological individuation, what remained outside his jurisdiction —the otherness of wildness (internal and external), death, and the mysteries of growth and decay—would be repressed by his anxious fears, and this, too, would push him back toward those ready-made defenses that protect the infant from his own helplessness: unconscious fantasies and projections. These would disguise the wild beasts with his own ferocity and mask the tame with his yearning and vulnerability.

As the infant normally grows away from being ruled by his stomach, the new farmers and their artisan neighbors were increasingly ruled by the collective stomach. To become so absorbed with the auguries and techniques of food production gives a final ironic twist to their departure from the totemic culture that faded as farming increased. The totemic thinker mused on the classification of plants and the behaviors of animals, on food relations and food chains, and translated his impressions through the idiom of mythopoetic thought to marriage and kin relationships. Thus it was that the endless patterns of nature as food were scrutinized with infinite care as signs and markers, as the language of human relatedness. The farmer's literal preoccupation with food is like a parody of the taxonomic collections of the child, who wants endlessly to know the names of things, who is, so to speak, storing away elements of concrete reality from which to create a world. For the child and farmer, those things seem to be an end in themselves, whereas in true maturity they are only the beginnings of thought. The farmer spends more time engrossed with the future, imagining tomorrow and its possible prodigality or paucity. It is as though the human capacity for absorbing mythic stories as personal psychodrama had played the mean trick of stranding the dreamer in endless accountability for tomorrows, some of which would inevitably be disastrous.[26]

An individual unsure of the distinctions between himself and his nonhuman surroundings accepts such an awesome duty, thrust upon him by his own blending of his identity with the landscape, positing it in priesthoods and churches. For him, to be in control of the fertility of the soil is desperately bound to his person in an autistic envelope. Such was the farmer's and villager's monolithic view of a dependent symbiosis with a Mother Earth. Such a dyadic concept might alleviate the heaped-up, duty-bound, guilt-laden burden, saturating the relationship with ecstatic adoration and contentment. But in her cruel moments of dearth that mother would be worse than any dangerous beast, and the memory of that painful episode would leave its schizoid print on everyone in society, scars that the bountiful harvest could not erase.

The care of crops, stock, and children fixed the daily routine and increased the amount of work. Like casual gathering or preambles to the chase, the work was probably light in the earliest centuries of planting, but in time it would take everything. The world of drudgery would eventually seem normal, the savage would be scorned for his indolence and lack of expectant suspense, and the only escape for tillage or bureaucratic time-serving would be death. These anxieties would elicit a certain satisfaction in repetitive and exhausting routines reminiscent of the swayings of the autistic child or the rhythmic to-and-fro of the captive bear or elephant in the zoo. Early farming represents a "state of surrender," says anthropologist Daphne Prior, and the farmer was a defeated captive.[27]

Like a prisoner of war, he would survive if he could psy-

43

chologically adapt. As for relishing monotony, where is one to find the developmental precursors to the workaday world? We have already touched on the food conservatism of the adolescent, which, in fact, is only one detail of a much broader mind-set. The strictures apply as well to clothing, daily routines, catchwords, and circle of friends—a powerful pubertal resurgence of childish clinging, the two-year-old's clutching familiar places like a limpet, hating trips and strangers and new tastes. He wants his accustomed stories and toys: woe to the liberal parent who, supposing that "creativity" is primed only by novelty, takes an insecure child on a long vacation, for the parent will be punished and chagrined by the clamor for familiar things, home, and the same old books read exactly in the same way.

Probably these rejections of strangeness play a healthy role in the normal stages of the life cycle: among nomadic hunter-foragers, they may keep small children from wandering too far; in the young child, the reluctance to adventure may be part of consolidating gains already made in a strange new world; among adolescents, conformity solidifies loyalties as the subadults approach the limbo of nonbelonging between childhood and grownup status. But clinging conformity is an appropriate model for maturity only if the problems of the child or adolescent remain unresolved, as they do in the children of parents who themselves are psychologically troubled and inept.[28] For the child in such a family, the unremitting infantile behaviors and psychopathic modes to which they lead are adaptive: they are the means for surviving defective home environments and, ultimately, for surviving distorted world views. But they do not lead toward psychological maturity, a view broad and forgiving, recognizing the limits of membership and the importance of selfhood within the group —like that of Chiefs Seattle and Smallahala, who saw the invading whites as wrong and yet as human. Such an attitude, it seems to me, involves a sense of the larger gift of life, a realistic perception of the self and the Other, and a sense of the talents of generosity and circumspection, all of which were at odds with the needs of the early village craftsman, on whom the domesticated world imposed the framework of rewards, competition, and exclusiveness, hoarding of seed strains, rejection of cross-tribal marriage, and abandonment of the metaphysical potency of all creatures for the utility of a few. Loyalty and conformity were absolutely central, enkindled in the callow human fears of foreign ways and non-belonging.

Of course, this generalized description of the farmer/villager is used as a mode; there are exceptions. The loving acceptance of the strangeness of life, the wit to become fully oneself and yet not estranged from the infinite diversity of the Other, the leisured, free openness to self-unfolding instead of clinging to a made world may indeed be achieved by the individual farmer who knows birdsong as well as the cackling hen, who gathers and fishes as well as plants and cultivates. On the subsistence farm of nineteenth-century Illinois, in sixteenth-century Flanders, at the homesteads of ancient Celt wheatcrofters, as among the first inhabitants of Jericho, such leisure may have been possible—as it may be anywhere on rich uncrowded soils in favorable climates. The final phases of maturity, in which the seasoned individual becomes capable of mentorship and spiritual guidance, are in some degree within reach of all in such places.

The Near Eastern human habitats at the end of the Ice Age were also rich and fruitful, and the earliest planters may have been as much the beneficiaries of the full cycle of individual psychogenesis as their ancestors and their farmer heirs on the fruitful soils of the north. But the land changed. Subarid desert fringes are especially vulnerable to both abuse and climate. Men were forced to find in their own psychological

45

makeup the resources to meet the demands of the domestic community in an ecologically deteriorating world. Slowly and without planned intent, the subjective experience changed in its equilibrium with the external world. In Freudian terms, the id or instinctive impulses as the expression of instinctual wildness became synonomous with the desert; the ego came to attend more and more to human products; and the social matrix of the superego grew in focus and complexity.

But no Freudian terms are needed to see that village life put demands on the minds of adults that resembled distorted versions of the growing pains of typical children of *Homo sapiens* everywhere. Perhaps the greater complexity of life in village society did not actually counterbalance the simplification of the nonhuman environment. Thus, the difference between the psychological world of the adult and the child in the villages was not as great as that between adults and children among the ancestral hunters. This is not what one expects from the traditional view of history. But history itself, an idea accounting for a made world, was invented by villagers as a result of five thousand years of strife and struggle to hold environment and self together. As a simplistic, linear, literal account of events and powers as unpredictable as parental anger, history is a juvenile idea.

3

The Desert Fathers

—

IF IDEAS HAVE HABITATS in which they originate and prosper, then the desert edge might be called the home of Western thought. Historically this is common knowledge, for the peoples of the dry landscapes of Egypt, Sumer, Assyria, Palestine, and the Eastern European and Eurasian borders of the Mediterranean Sea fashioned many of the concepts that define Occidental civilization.

To understand this aridity of culture we must stand apart from the conventions of history, even while using the record of the past, for the idea of history is itself a Western invention whose central theme is the rejection of habitat. It formulates experience outside of nature and tends to reduce place to location. To it, the plains and passes of the desert fringe are only a stage upon which the human drama is enacted. History conceives the past mainly in terms of biography and nations. It seeks causality in the conscious, spiritual, ambitious character of men and memorializes them in writing.[1]

The desert is a powerful, unique sensorium. Silence and emptiness are the ambiguous descriptions of sounds and landforms. The desert is at once a place of sensory deprivation and awesome overload—too little life, too much heat, too little water, too much sky. Its cool shadows offer "thermal delight," and yet the desert evokes the terrors of the inferno.[2]

Its distance and scale, the sweep between horizons and the loftiness of stars, its winds and mirages, its hidden life and conspicuous shapes seem at once to dwarf and to emphasize the human figure. Its sensory impact is profoundly stimulating and disturbing, a massive shock to the human limbic system—the neural basis of emotional response—which seems to demand some logic or interpretation.

Between the senses and the logic is perception—that is, the biopsychological screening devices, filters, combined forces of inherent tendency and individual experience that direct attention and focus possibilities. Thus, what the desert means is preceded by preconscious selection of what is seen and how it is seen. Myriad qualities of the desert beg for interpretation: the firmness of outline; the linearity of horizon and movement; the separateness of things and their static, fixed quality as though made by some absent artisan; the way light and dark, sky and earth, life and death insist on contrast and duality; the ephemerality of creatures and transience of man; the flickering vitality of things distant, such as the planets; things unseen but heard, opposed to the frozen immobility of stone. These are some of the preconscious pointers toward interpretation.

Although it seems inimical to human life, the desert—the great dry belts that straddle the Tropics of Cancer and Capricorn—is the home of the world's civilizations. At the waterholes and along the rivers of the arid subtropics of Asia, Africa, and Europe where the three continents join, history began—not in the sandy desert proper, but at its edges. These margins are not desert habitats proper, but ecological *ecotones*. They include the spare shrub communities at the fringe of sandy plains or stony plateaus; the patches of grassland on slightly moister slopes; traces of savanna; the evergreen dry forest of the mountain islands; the verdant park and wetlands of the oases and river margins proper; and the derelict phases of all such vegetative communities degenerating toward barren rock as a result of climatic change and human abuse.

It was never the occupation of desert that mattered, but its isolating effects. It began with dramatic suddenness at the edges of valleys where cultivation and settlement leave off, always reminding farmers and their urban cousins of the separation of fertility and barrenness. The desert of the Near East was once the home of wild animals, barbarian nomads, and mounted invaders from the east and north, with whom settled peoples also engaged in commerce.

Village, town, and city life in the great valleys, as understood from the archaeological record, was a stew of seventy centuries of turmoil and havoc as well as building and growth. Recurring disasters are evident in their litter, often including the downfall of the great theocratic cities. Their ruins, numbering more than a hundred, are among the great spectacles of the earth. City after city was built upon the decimated foundations of its predecessors. Today scores of tiny villages squat on the shattered wreckage of centers that once contained many thousands of inhabitants. The pattern of expansion and collapse emerging from the excavations of these ruins is one of rising power and prosperity followed by environmental deterioration and social catastrophe, the fateful tides of powerful theocracies made vulnerable by their own success.

The cycle typically began with the concentration of authority and organization expressed in warlike expansion, territoriality, and the engineering of water supplies and irrigation. The amount of productive soil was increased by the carefully managed distribution of water. Gradually irrigation became extended complex hydraulic systems. As the population exceeded its available resources, emigrants went upstream on the heels of timber cutters and charcoal makers, many settling as stockkeepers in the watersheds of the tributaries of mainstreams like the Tigris and Euphrates. Over the years, their livestock increased and denuded and trampled the slopes, destroying their vegetative cover and soil. The land lost its water-retaining capacity, increasing the runoff after rains and reducing the groundwater supplies in springs and wells. The seasonal variation in water supply was exaggerated by this flooding and scarcity. Silt threatened to clog the impoundments and the miles of intricate water-feeder systems upon which the agriculture depended.[3]

Cultivation, once it reached the limits of tillable land, was intensified. Crop specialization, control of weeds and pests, and increased intensity of demand on the soil set the stage for periodic outbreaks of crop diseases and invasions of pests and parasites whose wild foods were gone. Nutrient-element deficiencies and soil salination also helped set the stage for debacle.

As chiefdoms were swallowed by kingdoms and kingdoms confronted other kingdoms, defense put heavy demands on manpower, straining the bureaucratic management of the land. The semi-isolation of the great city-states converted the whole region into a giant experiment in communicable human diseases, so that, in spite of his resistance to contaminated food and water, to local strains of bacteria, viruses, nematodes, and flatworms, the citizen of such a state became vulnerable to new forms of diseases brought by traders and invaders.

Thus emerged the Four Horsemen of the Apocalypse: conscription, enslavement, famine, and disease.[4] Cataclysms of whatever kind were followed by hydraulic failure and mud deposits so suffocating that neither conquerors nor stragglers could easily renew the buried waterworks that had taken decades or even centuries to build. Eventually a new city would emerge, a cult and power center of the district. Its inhabitants, like their predecessors, would seek the ritual protection of their gods, whose connection with the earth and its seasons entailed a mythology of the soil and its autochthonous forces, of the springs and streams, the weather, and the secrets of germination. They would try harder to harmonize their society with the powers of nature. But they too would fail.[5]

Since the tempo of this cycle of catastrophe and renewal was in terms of many lifetimes, it was probably more or less invisible to those who lived it. A record-keeping observer, an interested hovering alien, however, might see the futility and illusory security even though he might not recognize its ecological aspects. Most desert tribesmen were disengaged, but they were not so analytic or so interested. Another watcher from the desert was the self-styled outcast. By self-definition the Hebrews were the "outsiders." Although they adopted a nomadic style, the Hebrews were never true outsiders and contemptuous of the city in the manner of Arab nomads. Hangers-on at the fringe, mixing scorn and yearning, the little tribes of placeless people perceived with keen and biting insight the folly of the great pagan theocracies that worshipped the wrong gods.

On the most ambitious scale in the history of the world, the ancestors of the Old Testament made virtue of their homelessness. They struck a gold vein of moral analysis by assimilating certain themes of transience from genuine nomads while rejecting their fatalism. In a Semitic storm god they found a traveling deity who was everyplace and therefore not bound by location. Owning nothing, they created a theology of contingent divinity, and heroic escape.

The Hebrews discovered and occupied a force field of human relations that has been one of the most distinctive features of the Near and Middle East from the time of the earliest agriculture: the gap between pastoralist and farmer. The farmer was economically and politically allied with the

city. The domestication of plants and animals led to a Neolithic dialectic, a split in husbandry between pastorality and
tillage. This Cain and Abel motif is deep in the blood of
Western origins. It is fundamental to the ideological psychology of "us" against "them" that the desert seemed always to
echo in its physical contrasts.

Although basically economic, the dialectic resonated with
other dualities. What to their ancestral hunter-gatherers had
been a polar equilibrium whereby men hunted and women
gathered was sundered into masculinist and patriarchal societies of animal breeders on the one hand and Great Mother–
worshiping, plant-tending cultivators of the soil on the other.

City and country were not then the symbols of opposition,
but allies against the wandering peoples of the desert. The
mythology of the ancient city-states was profoundly imbued
with feminine principles and dominated by pantheons of powerful goddesses. Central to religion were the cosmic cycle of
life, the sacredness of soil and water, the spirituality of particular places, and reverence for seasonal rhythms and harmo-
nies of growth and decay, birth and death. These values were
shared by the craftsmen, tradesmen, bureaucrats, and others
of the city, centered there in a temple priesthood.

Pastoralists have traditionally shown distaste for a life of
manure shoveling, mucky sluice reaming, and the drudgery
and passivity of tending and waiting. To this adopted attitude
the critical and analytic Hebrew added a revulsion for the
heterodoxy of the city's foreign traffic, with its bastardizing,
accommodating, and polluting of religion and invidious pursuit of vanity and money. It seemed apparent to the Hebrew
prophets that false gods, wantonness, and materialism destined all such centers to destruction. True pastoralists might
have agreed, turned their backs and gone their way, but the
Hebrews watched and learned from the crack in the dialectical
world. Outside the city gates, self-exiled, deriding those in-

side, sharpening new powerful weapons of objective analysis, they formulated a *via negativa*. The inevitable catastrophes that had left ruins in every direction since the beginnings of civilization testified to an inevitable providential nemesis. God was just, as well as distant from all this ritual elaboration and collaboration between men and the soil. It was not any particular Mesopotamian myth that was wrong; it was myth itself.

So the Hebrews did not choose pastoral myths, although they incorporated pastoral style: patriarchal authoritarianism, the principle of mobility, durability, frugality, a penchant for abstraction and distancing, a conscious disengagement. The giver and maker and destroyer would topple all walls and priests and kings at times and by means of his own choosing, not as the manifestation of the outraged divinity incarnate in things, but as an unknowable master outside of the creation. The occasion of all his acts would escape prediction and cyclic formats; his means would be his own: flood, famine, plague, invasion. The spectacular pattern of ruins around them told nothing of the when and how of calamity. Nothing about ordinary experience could inform one about such a god.

The Hebraic ideal was an extraordinary ambition: self-styled exiles, fugitives, wanderers, a community of alienated souls who disavowed both the substance and form of the bonding ties by which men had acknowledged kinship with earth and tribe from the dawn of consciousness and which they had given form in the exemplary and metaphorical model of myth. The ancient notion of the multiplicity of truth, of hidden spirit in all things; the mystic simultaneity of past, present, and future; the credence in spoken, sung, carved, drawn, or danced affirmation of the cohesion of all things; the reading of nature as the divine language: all were seen as illusory in the eyes of the chosen prophets and chosen people.

The Hebrews understood that, however comprehensible

natural events might be in their own right, they were meaningless in any cosmic sense. While the world was still to be revered as belonging to Him, it was to be understood that He did not regularly speak through the mysteries of birth, growth, death, the beauty and variety of life, the mutual ties among natural and social forms, or by means of incarnate, numinous hierophantic objects.

The Hebrews invented a special myth that denied the message of regularity and causal interconnectedness that had been the stuff of pagan myth. The human psyche was still to be nurtured with stories—not accounts of analogical beginnings uniting present and past, but of origins actually distant in time; not familiar oral recitations or rhetorical episodes of an epic, but quotations from the written word; not affirming a methectic, but rather a cathartic world where estrangement was the condition of all men. Just as the ancient Hebrew lived in the crevice of the Neolithic split, Occidental men would come to see themselves as neither wholly spiritual nor wholly natural, as fragmented rather than plural in nature.

The new antimythological myth was history. Psychologically it served as all myths do: as a story of the past that explains origins, establishes exemplary models of behavior, and provides the conventions of a particular group. Yet it was psychologically dysfunctional in order to sustain the ideal of estrangement. Its most revolutionary aspect was its repudiation of the cyclic pattern of events, its insistence on the truly linear flow of time, and its pursuit of its own abstract, self-confirming truth as opposed to indicators and signs in the concrete world.

Because historical events were unique, they were not analogous to the body, family, or natural processes. They were interpreted by envoys, through words written rather than spoken, proclamations tinged with strangeness, a kerygmatic, or preaching and prophetic, form. The evangelical assertion of the new Word was not intended to make man fit into the world, but to verify his isolation and emphasize the unpredictability and disjunction of experience.[6] Where traditional myths had been part of a great man-culture-nature-divine cybernetics, the new myth extolled the mystery of God's purpose and the discontinuity of events.

Even its linear pattern gave minimal form. Unlike the cosmological matrices of Neolithic culture, historical progression was at best a broken point-to-point sequence, full of random turns, like literary fiction. In contrast to the satisfactions of a universal harmony, it had only a lean and bare claim that things happened, but expressed little of their "whatness." It was conducive to a skepticism previously unknown. It favored a new attitude of self-scrutiny and uprooted the temptation to close with the visible world or to accept it as an expression of divinity. Life was a sensuous snare, alluring with intimations of a centered reality on earth, full of spurious signs of purpose. The doubting, sometimes mocking, rummaging, questioning attitude toward the world was extended also to a new inward scrutiny. It would reveal the artificiality of all culture and the selfishness of human motives, not only the self-delusion in all explanation, but the frailty of criticism itself.

To observe that this renovation of consciousness took place at the edge of the desert is not to say that it was caused by the desert. Perhaps it is not possible to separate causes and evidence at the level of preconscious perception. Such a consciousness might include attention habitually directed to the sky, the relative insignificance of all things organic, the sense of hidden, invisible, unknowable power that seems more akin to the wind than to concrete things. Waiting, silence, emptiness, and nothingness seem to imprint themselves on the concept of truth, self, ultimate states. In general, none of the great world religions is life affirming. They all seem to dislo-

TWO VIEWS OF LIFE:

———————Myth———————

	Myth (col 1)	Myth (col 2)
The Nature of Life	Eternal and recurring patterns, to which fertility and fatality are crucial, hence death is positive and recyclic. Time is synchronous: the past and future are enfolded in the present. Metamorphosis is central but oriented to stability rather than change. Nothing is fortuit-	ous. The principles of totality, predictability and regularity are important. Nature and culture are in sacred symbiosis; alien cultural systems are merely different expressions of that same embeddedness. Man is at home in the world.
The Earth and the Cosmos	God takes multiple forms and the sacred appears in all areas of life. Nature has many clues to divinity, and there also exists a culture-divinity continuum. God embodies institutions, and in them shrines, forms, images and art are	central. Life reanimates a larger cosmographic scheme. Man participates in this according to an epigenetic level of responsibility. Terrain forms, graves, and other sacred places reflect telluric and autochthonous forces.
The Basis of Knowing	All men possess an oral preunderstanding, an intuition extending from their own bodies. Mnemonic thought is applied to an analyzable world in an avidity for parallels, ritually enacted and celebrated. Science is concrete, enlarging meaning; nature offers clues to logos. Binary speculation and sys-	tems of difference are fundamental. Metaphor is the mode of divine access; forms are metaphors of powers. Myth is inseparable from ideology and morality. The record is mythopoetic, oral and musical. Estrangement of the individual is only an interval in an integrative rite.

cate and abstract *as though* taking some sign from the insignificance of life in the overwhelming geometry of mineral and astronomical forces around them. "The desert," says Herbert Schneidau in his *Sacred Discontent,* was "the concrete image of transcendence" appropriate to an unknowable God, though not his home—something "wholly other," a place of contrasting, negating oppositions.[7]

MYTH AND HISTORY*

───────────History───────────

		The Nature of Life
Emphasis is on the diachronicity and linear change in time. The world is more provisional, contingent and even random in its patterns. The purpose of life is not evident in nature, so that nature and culture are either opposed or categorized as science and history. Strangeness, estrangement and	fragmentation are characteristic. Doctrines and cults rise and fall; other cultures are mocked as erroneous. Masculine and feminine seem to be opposing. Society sees itself as nomadic, pastoral and patriarchal. The causes and purposes of things are not inherent in them.	
God is apart from the world and institutions, including art and culture. God is arbitrarily unlocalized and his actions are intrusive, unexpected interruptions. Events are linked in disparate strata of time	God is not in nature, nor is truth multiple. Guilt and a sense of deserved disaster are part of the "thouness" of history. Myth is seen as a shield from the truth.	The Earth and the Cosmos
Understanding is dialectical, Platonic or ideological. God gives messages to chosen spokesmen, and they are not repeated. Kinship is less important than chosenness. Meaning comes from prophecy or dramatic, broken, probing, or literary interpretation. Metaphor	and ritual and art are peripheral. All meaning is precarious and unique. "The beginning" has literal rather than homological significance. Personal effects are skepticism, alienation, and self-analysis.	The Basis of Knowing

*Based on Herbert Schneidau, *Sacred Discontent*, Berkeley: University of California Press, 1977.

Its emptiness, as Aldous Huxley observed, is conducive to concentration, hallucination, sensory deprivation, spiritual exaltation, madness, and death.[8] Its desolation is the vestment of those who want no home on earth and find a solacing humility in their own nothingness and liberation from the body. For some, the desert quest is to resolve discontinuity and seek an ultimate unity. For the Egyptians, along the predictable Nile, stability, symmetry, and coherence ruled the cosmos. For the Hebrew fathers, however, there was no afterlife, no access to God beyond prayer, and no intrinsic order on earth.

History is a collective memory of the past which denies the telluric dimension of place. History was the only way to keep myth while holding that the desert was no more than a stage.[9] Eventually its authoritarian, masculinist, ascetic ideology would spread into the cities themselves, defeating the feminine mysteries associated with riverine and oasis agriculture, a victory for transcendence over the natural and indigenous.

Though important to the roots of Western spiritual life, the desert for the Hebrews was not valued as a place. It was a vacuum, idealized as a state of disengagement and alienation, a symbol of the condition of the human spirit. Its physiological potency for visionary ecstasy is evident in the lives of holy men, from the prebiblical patriarchs to Moses, Jesus, Mohammed, and thousands of pilgrims, hermits, monks, and their followers.[10]

This purist or puritan heritage ranges throughout Western religious inspiration, an idealism constantly threatened by the telluric powers of heathen cults, as irrepressible as weeds. However much seasonal festival and mythic intuition the Jew and Christian clung to in their daily lives, the dominant thrust of the West was, at bottom, estrangement and abstraction.[11]

Perhaps something of the same can be said for monotheism itself. As theory, it persists with the capacity to outlive and undercut liturgical practices. Like the demythologized world, a one-God cosmos may be beyond the sustained capacity of the normal individual. "The creed of Sinai tore up the human psyche by its most ancient roots," writes George Steiner. God became as "blank as the desert air," and "the Judaic summons to perfection" was so impossible as to be a "blackmail of transcendence."[12] Steiner attempts to account for the persecution of the Jew and the Holocaust as examples of the periodic outbursts of revenge against the originators of monotheism.

What is it about human psychology that finds monotheism intolerable? David Miller believes that polytheistic religious experience means being gripped by a story in which the diversity of the many characters is "the symbolic expression of a lively process." The gods and goddesses "teach us an acceptance of the variousness of ourselves and others." The monotheistic search for a single sense of identity makes us feel guilty for not getting it all together, which is impossible in a plural universe. Thinking is polytheistic, "a reality in which truth and falsity, life and death, beauty and ugliness, good and evil are forever and inextricably mixed together." The powers and forces are dramatically revealed in an acceptable way. The story form keeps what James Hillman calls "the feeling function" alive, harmonizing the "in here" with the "out there."[13]

If he cannot find evidence for a single center in a diverse world, the monotheist feels lost, experiences a disconnectedness, and senses the "death of God," which is to say, the deadness of abstraction. Belief divorced from tangible support is tiring, dull, out of touch. Theology becomes "irrelevant to faith and philosophy irrelevant to everything." Miller concludes that monotheism socially becomes fascism, imperialism, or capitalism; philosophically is unmetaphorical, unambiguous, and dichotomous; and psychologically is rigid, fixed, and linear.

Miller's polytheism in the service of a lively narrative contains not simply a heterogeneous collection of gods, but a sequence of "worlds of being and meaning in which my personal life participates." These are not merely reflected aspects of the psyche, but the means by which thought is divinized and the earth sacralized, modeling not a one-and-many but a multivalenced world. History, however plural, is not concerned with multiple bases of an ongoing creativity or the spiritual significance of concrete diversity, but with an account of events subordinated to a single divinity. It is, says Miller, inadequate as an explanation for the way our experience actually feels; it does not link up coherently. Out of our desperation we grasp at any center that gives pattern and meaning. Ideology is born: dialectic belief, religious or secular, that fills a vacuum in the absence of religious enculturation based on lifelong immersion, with its preunderstanding continuously confirmed by sensory experience and the logic of natural relationships.

Ideology, according to Louis J. Halle, is ultimately defined as the "us against them" mentality.[14] It is the expression, often social, of an implacable and irrational dualism. It is especially powerful in desert lands because the desert seems to confirm a law of oppositions to the senses, despite ideology's own scorn for such natural reference. The "cradle of civilization" is also the cradle of fanatic ideology—witness the interminable wars, large and small, that boil across its deserts. The ideologist pursues not only an idea to live by but to die and kill for, horribly distorting juvenile loyalty to kin and adolescent conformity and idealism. Perhaps this is the meaning of Kenneth Rexroth's snort that "the entire Judeo-Christian-Muslim period in human history has been an episode of unparalleled perceived and social psychosis and international barbarity."[15]

The logic that blames the Hebrews who invented monotheism for all its effects is, of course, unreasonable. The Christians, the Persian cults, the Platonic-Aristotelian Greeks, and the Dark Ages of Europe worked the idea toward its bitter ends. At first, the payoff of the Hebrew prophetic tradition, like that of all minority extremists, had been security, in spite of the felt impotence. It required centuries of devoted effort to realize the either/or possibilities of monotheism, and the desert fringes as its appropriate setting. Paradise before the Fall, Paul's rapture, and the celestial realm all became interchangeable, as opposed to the real world, the desert, which represented sin, according to Basil (d. 379) and Gregory (d. 390). Persian duality helped the Christians transform all ambiguity into opposition instead of metaphor. The efforts of religious energy to reanimate the cosmos merely had the effect thereafter of creating sides, populated with demons and devils on one hand and saints and angels on the other. Augustine saw the desert itself as a war. Animals represented evil. The anchorites, like their modern fundamentalist heirs, were eager to fight devils "in the freedom of the vast wilderness," according to John Cassian (d. 435), in order "to find that life which can be compared to the bliss of angels." The hermit-animal traditions, involving Jerome (d. 420) and John the Baptist, meant subduing that ferocity which was supposed to have resulted from the Fall.

As the Testaments went northwest into Europe, so did the desert. Internalized after a thousand years, it became a necessary adjunct to evangelical desacralizing of place and to the demythologizing of the pagan tribes of the north. The concept of the wilderness became for the West the umbrella beneath which the divine discontent of the desert and the gothic fears of the northern forest could be lumped.[16] Christian evangelism would invent such sweeping condemnations of nature as the Christians progressed from a rural minority toward urban power and urban thinking.

The relationship of the desert environment to the Western myth of history, to monotheism and to ideology seems to invoke a debate about environmental determinism, but such a debate is no longer possible, for it was grounded in the defunct idea of the early twentieth Century that genetical inheritance and the experience of the individual were opposing or competing forces, that the history of culture had something to do with escape from instinct and nature. The real difficulty with the discussion of the relationship of history to place is that the question is framed in an historical mode which has already decided the issue. History is inimical to compliance with nature, having arisen in a tragic perspective of man against nature, or nature as neutral. Using nature as a parable of politics, it sees all events in ideological texts.[17] Determinism is itself a linear, causal concept, an historical rather than cybernetic way of thinking. It is as though it were invented in order to overstate the role of natural control in human matters, which are then seen, in reaction, as matters of choice, chance or supernatural intervention.

The Hebrew inventors of history did perceive accurately: the earth gods did not save the Sumerians from recurring disaster. Why now should we therefore find their transcendental vision any more at fault than that of the cybernetic, mythic peoples? Certainly not directly on ecological grounds. A score of Neolithic cultures decimated the ecosystems they occupied in spite of their attunement to the seasons, to the auguries of plants and animals, and to their rituals of soil and place. It is ontogeny rather than ecology of which we must speak.

What the desert fathers—in the form of history, Hebrews, patriarchs and monotheists—did to the ontogeny of the person must be seen in the context of the swaths already cut by agriculture. Those were in the psychological debilitations of diminished maternal care in large families and in the loss of wildness and otherness from the juvenile's world. The desert fathers, like their Arabic, pastoral models, scourged adolescence. They could amputate and cauterize pubertal epigenesis because they would further transform the relationship of the infant to its mother.

Having taken the desert vacancy as its sensorium and the

nomadic pastoralist Arabs as paradigmatic fathers, the Hebrews and their spiritual cousins could not have escaped the
consequences. For example, the price of patriarchy is that it
"denies to the woman and the child any weight, any autonomy, and any reality. The only serious world is that of the
adult male. . . . It is the function of social customs and rites
which surround birth, weaning, circumcision, excision—all
forms of passage, in short—to prolong this fact, to accentuate
it, to acknowledge it—or rather, on the contrary, to conjure
it away, to liquidate it, and to make all traces of it disappear.
. . . The world of mothers will be buried in the depths of an
idealized past, and enveloped in fantasies. . . . This is what
permits the unmasking of nature's mysteries and the decod-
ing of her signs, as well as the annulment of the prohibitions
which cover nature," says A. Bouhdiba on Arab-Muslim society.[18]

Landscapes, in such an abstract world, tend to become
symbols of ideas. George Williams has traced out the transformation of "wilderness" and "paradise" into states of mind.
The Puritans, especially the Protestants, made much of the
idea of paradise. The word itself comes from the Persian for
"garden" and is a forerunner of the idea of utopia. It has been
interpreted as a Muslim expression of a land of "instinctual
gratification" dominated by the pleasure principle.[19] For the
Christians, its ambiguity works its way into the very center of
the idea of the Fall, in which their scorn for sensual gratification, as experienced by Adam, marks their swing toward repression. But the ambiguity about paradise was there long
before the first Christian.

The over-mothered infant in patriarchal society and,
among boys, their severance from the world of women ex-
ploits the theorizing openness of the adolescent. In him the
dream of paradise will be nourished by that loss and will feed
his fantasies and his hopes for the future. Its emotional inten-

sity will also heat the opposite of paradise, the wilderness. Yet the two, in their polarity, have analogous points in purity and remoteness, in their romantic perfection. The quality of this remote yet yearned-for purity is native to the state of adolescence itself, and bears to adolescence a functional psychological role.

Peter Blos, Norman Kiell, Anna Freud, Erik Erikson, and many others have described the characteristic subjectivity and behavior of adolescence. Perhaps the most peculiar of these features is a regression to certain infantile traits: playfulness with sound making and word meanings; body sensibilities and self-consciousness; "acting out" of feelings and emotions; extreme variability and instability of moods; a reinvigorated fraternal and paternal attachment; and fantasies of power and heroics. In addition, the adolescent typically is preoccupied with larger questions: the meaning and purpose of life; concepts of infinity, space, time, and God; and the ideal human relationship and community. Piaget speaks of this as a formal or abstract level; others call it symbolic thought.

Much of this is familiar and common knowledge. Yet, in a historical-existentialist society the right questions may not be asked. Adolescent behavior can be made to seem a response to the circumstances in which a youth finds himself: the uncertainty and choices faced by the subadult; the somewhat irresponsible status granted him by adults; and the ambivalent experience of being between childhood and maturity, like a melon not quite ripe.

In the light of human evolution, however, the adolescent traits can be seen not only as symptoms of a growth spurt or as adjustments to social limbo, but as a highly specialized process of emergence. In small-group, tribal societies, adolescence is perceived as a gestation followed by the birth of the adult. The whole group is intimately involved in this process. Mircea Eliade, the eminent scholar of comparative religions, has described its basic format, even though its details vary among different societies: the ceremonial death of the child, the acquisition of new skills and knowledge, the new capacity to endure and suffer, rites of rebirth in initiation, and a vision quest. Central to these administrations is attention to his indigenous desire for cosmic understanding and profound devotion.[20] Because his comprehension of the religious significance and origins of life can only be grasped metaphorically, the language of these ultimate matters is mythopoetic, based on metaphors from concrete experience, especially, says Joseph Campbell, the "imprints of infancy."

The adolescent becomes psychologically infantlike on his own in order to be reborn culturally as an adult. Each of the infantile behaviors lends itself in some appropriate way to this transition. The so-called primary thought and infantile self-centeredness of the first months of life serve as a state of mind from which wider relationships are developed, as they will be again in adolescence, on a new plane. It is not the infant's fantasy of omnipotence or its love/hate feelings toward its mother, but its movement beyond that duality that is crucial to the successful outcome of adolescence. Graduation from the mother matrix into the larger sphere of a maternal earth matrix in early childhood is the basis for good, concrete object relationships and is also part of the later adolescent graduation exercise into adult status. The wordplay and poetry-mindedness of the adolescent and his new sensitivity to symbolic thought moves him away from the classifications of concrete reality—of animals, plants, weather, rocks, planets, and water—that had been the central tasks of speech in childhood.

Like land birds instinctively setting out on transoceanic migration, given assurance, so to speak, from the experience of the species that there is land on the other side, the human adolescent organism reenters the dangerous ground of immature perception on the premise that society is prepared to meet his psychic demands for a new landing—that is, that society is organized to take these refractory youths through a powerful, tightly structured gestation; to test, teach, reveal; to offer as Erikson says, things worthy of their skill; to tutor their suffering and dreaming; and to guide their feelings of fidelity. If the infancy to which they look for an exemplary protocol of growth has been blighted, or if the adult group is not prepared to administer the new and final birth, then the youths create autistic solutions to their own needs and, prolonging the quest of their adolescence, sink finally, cynically, back into their own incompetent immaturity, like exhausted birds going down at sea.

The scenario created by Western cultures was different, however. The kind of society sought by the Hebrew prophets repudiated the nature-lore parts of a developmental process by which maternal connections are subjectively transferred to the earth, subsequently locking them into the intense idealism of adolescence without the intermediary experience of belonging to Mother Earth. The loss of mother thwarts a middle factor, plunging the individual forever into infantile dualism, without a connecting ground that melts the alternatives of either hating the protective, nourishing She who abandoned him or fixedly adoring the feminine in the guise of his own mother's face, to the detriment of his capacity to establish a mature relationship with the other sex or with any Other. This prolonged, crippling disease of attention and the fantasies of omnipotence as they ripen in adolescent idealism perhaps more than any other traits mark the desert-fringe civilizations.

This faulty developmental scenario separates society from the rhythms of natural life and substitutes a critical posture toward all schematizing. Events erupt into history. There is no preunderstanding in the Hebraic prophetic archetype of fiction, in Attic probing of tragedy, in Socratic isolation, or in

Greek self-scrutiny. In time, art and science became data making instead of tools in myth and ritual. Fictional literature, the art form most peculiar to the descendents of the desert mind, is, says Herbert Schneidau, a defamiliarizing, dissolving solvent that, unlike myth, has a unique plot development, and end, as well as an individual author and point of view. It is, like history, a probe that deconstructs, serving ideology in its verification by conviction.

The one-sided domination of Western cultural style by masculine values is typical of mounted nomadic peoples and was adopted and reformulated by the Hebrew fathers. Their sexual chauvinism is more or less true of the Neolithic as a whole. Even though the sedentary societies of the ancient world (including that side of Hebrew life) were locked in wonder at the powerful mysteries of place and soil, they were politically dominated by males.

The alternatives of male- or female-centered philosophy may seem in our time to be ideological forces to be adjusted by education, but their respective ascendency waxes and wanes in the psychological development of the child. In traditional tribal peoples, the prepubertal youth is commonly separated from his mother in order to undergo a new birth designed by men, as the first was by women, with the goal of moving the candidate toward a more holistic and polar complementarity between the sexes. It is the theme of this book that the individual is inherently mentally and emotionally tuned to those shifts in focus. The adolescent is prompted by his own intrinsic mood changes to be away from his mother's control. Then everything depends on what the mentors do, for they may, on the historical side, prolong, exaggerate, and make conscious an adult model derived from the pubertal child's tendency to dichotomize the sexes; or they may, on the mythic side, elaborate the separatism temporarily in order to further the purposes of an ultimate integration.[21] The novice's initiatory exercises and other educational experiences may strongly influence whether he proceeds psychologically and philosophically to a mature integration. Perhaps society and the individual are more vulnerable to an arrested development fixated on masculinity, rather than on femininity, for two reasons: first, the preoccupation with male forms and fathering is the last of alternated male/female phases before maturity; and, second, the physical domination of all societies by men can mislead the immature-minded into thinking that patriarchal values and ideals are synonymous with universal power.

The task of adolescence is to become whole at a new level of consciousness. The individual is deeply aware of this, though it is not clear to him what that means or how it is to be done. When teachers and counselors take him away from the household, they create the conditions in which the potential adult within him can be realized. But his new circumstances can mislead the individual into thinking that the changes that he feels to be urgent are to be made in the outer world. If in some way (such as the denial of the natural world as a language or the truncation of myth) the overall process is frustrated, the youth may remain stuck in the notion that his ideal can only be achieved by reforming the world.[22] Since any number of possible ways of doing that may be imagined, each supported by verbal logic, he is persuaded by his own limited judgment—first by one system of ideas, then another. His compulsion to succeed feeds mainly on his own sense of internal disharmony. Such an ideologist is a poor mentor, as he will perpetuate his own adolescent obsessions and thwarted rites of passage and guide his charges toward ideological choices.[23]

Because of his "fight with nature" the man of the desert must strike aggressively, says Watsuki Tetsuro.[24] After the model of the herdsman moving his flocks to wherever the grass is, the Westerner (like all men) enacts his own idea of the sacred in his life. A god, jealous and vengeful, who makes incursions into nature and human affairs is like the Arab herdsman or Assyrian horseman, sweeping things clear, testing his alliances. The fanatical idealist and his cynical alter ego see the world as a stage, fascinated by their self-image.[25]

To such pseudoequestrians the world is a designed set, says Lapham, speaking of this raiding aspect of our modern society in his essay, "The Melancholy Herd." Democracy is a "pastoral wandering through a department store" where expectations of power and wealth by the Bedouin-like American are like grass greening. Most noteworthy is the short span of attention, a transient-mindedness so dominated by moving on that even the modern city is merely a camp, its inhabitants fixated on change and fear of permanence. The transient mind is dominated by an interior desert of alienation, disappointment, self-hopelessness, and insignificance, for which war, prophecy, and visions are palliative. To those for whom wealth has literally sprung from the earth like milk from a teat, there is at best a poor sense of the cost of things, the value of work or of soil. Politics are like gossip, leadership inseparable from celebrity. The melancholy effect of all this is a hopeless desire for more than the world offers.[26]

Lapham portrays our aristocratic desert-mindedness as a catalog of childishness, a sort of amalgam of teenybopper frothiness and macho juvenile vapidity clearly not synonymous with the seriousness of the Hebrew desert fathers. They would have been scandalized at our scatterbrained yet patrician ignorance of history, our dabbling pursuit of entertainment and accumulation of things. Yet the similarity of Americans to mandarin Bedouins is neither accidental nor due to direct cultural heritage. It incorporates that body of adolescent traits and pastoral attitudes first assimilated into Western consciousness by Hebrew prophets and later reworked and secularized by Greek philosophers and modern Protestants. It is dominated by themes of alienation, disengagement, and unrelatedness—hence chaos.[27]

It is not my contention that the pubertal child (or, for that matter, the infant in whom the adolescent is immersed retroactively) is himself alienated; the ten-year-old with a moderately good nurturing is happily at home in the world. Gessell describes him in almost beatific terms. In the West, it is the failure of the adolescent's religious mentors in the succeeding four or five years to translate his confidence in people and the earth into a more conscious, more cosmic view, in which he broadens his buoyant faith to include the universe. The amputation of nature myths causes a grievous dislocation, for which he will seek, in true questing spirit, an explanation in terms of "ultimate" reality. He does not become an alienated person until he can give some logic to his flawed relationship to the world. The fiction granted him by the pseudopastoral desert philosophy of the West is that his painful incompleteness is the true mature experience and that the meaninglessness of the natural world is its meaning. In itself, this philosophy is merely inadequate, no worse than other intellectual dead ends. But, acted upon, it wounds us, and we wound the planet. The injury to normal individual development passed on to Western culture by Hebrew ascetics, their puritan emulators, and the Greek demythologizers persists at the root of our assumptions and attitudes about the world. The child's development is not aided by the intellectual masters of the West who control secondary education and are, in their turn, products and arbiters of a desolated adolescent quest.

The central dogma of the West insisted on a separation of spiritual matters from the phenomena of nature. Such a view is sustained not only by formal dogma, but by impairing the orchestrations of the growth of each generation. It is the philosophical expression of that phase of subadult life when the world seems abruptly altered and decentered, when the purposes of childhood have become irrelevant, and the bindings linking the adolescent as an adult to an awesome and complex new home are not yet perceived. Arrested at that point, denied the methectic workings and mythopoetic vision of man in nature, he will for the rest of his life struggle with existential problems that are normally the work of a few critical years in his second decade of life. I do not mean that the adolescent normally gains instant wisdom, but that the framework of nature as metaphoric foundation for cosmic at-homeness is as native to the human organism in its adolescent years as any nutritive element in the diet.

— Lacking it, he will always lack true reverence for the earth. The remaining choices for a logic of creation are an otherworldly orientation, materialist exploitation, or existentialist absurdity. The first calls upon an abstraction that lacks the psychological resources in the concrete, natural, named, and structured world of the juvenile matrix, the foundation for later metaphors, and regresses to the infant's schizoid fears of the loss of the good and bad mother. The second is fixated on juvenile literalness. The last builds its view upon a fragmented, meaningless world like that seen by the blind who are suddenly healed by surgery, like the barren, phenomenal world of the newborn.

In the developmental spiral of epigenesis, the clues to the meaning of things and events in each new matrix are in terms of those of the old. The landscape, for example, is given coherence by the preceding experience of the body and the mother's face, just as face and body had made sense in harmony with the rhythms, tastes, sounds, and cuddled comfort that were predicted by the womb. Biologically, this sequence proceeds to the final commencement, adolescent entry into a world of invisible realities anticipated by and including the physical terrain, its coherence emerging from the collective meanings that preceded it. Thus the normal regression of the adolescent at the brink of a mature vision revivifies and transforms the three archetypes—womb, body-face, and natural world. Each will in some way be available as images and reenactments by which his particular culture portrays the universe.

In Western pseudopastoralism, however, the desert is noplace; nature is a limbo (to the later puritans an evil snare). This view devastates the child's organizing work in two directions: it tends to diminish the potential of his understanding of social relationships by excluding the tangible nuances of events in nature that, by analogy, enrich early familial experience; and it sheds no symbolic light on the larger cosmos. The beneficiaries of eye surgery are usually subject to intense anxiety; the longer they have been blind, the more likely they are to abandon the pursuit of visual meaning and lapse into knowing by sound and touch.[28] Crawling babies explore the natural world joyously and fruitfully only if their mothers are reassuring and encouraging. If their mothers are overcautious and anxious, the child becomes fixated on the mother's emotion, reflects her fear and uncertainty, and instead of organizing a new matrix in the land, mechanically adopts the mother's fearful attitudes.[29]

The broken sequence of mental growth fostered by the fathers of the West cannot be represented simply as a bad link in an otherwise healthy chain. Unreconstructed adolescents make bad mothers and bad fathers. The parent whose oversimplified view of things places the natural world on a lower plane or in opposition to the social world will express this anxious, schizoid attitude in many ways to his children and will fail to make occasions for their own healthy growth beyond it. Humans intuitively see analogies between the concrete world out there and their own inner world. If they conceive the former as a chaos of anarchic forces or as dead and frozen, then so will they perceive their own bodies and society; so will they think and act on that assumption and vindicate their own ideas by altering the world to fit them; and so will they rear their children.

4

The Puritans

T HE CONCEPTS, ILLUSIONS, AND DREAMS about nature
that mark Protestant thought are not, to me, comprehensible
in terms only of the Reformation. Those notions saturate the
modern world; its radio preachers, newspaper editorialists,
and corporate warlocks alike make pronouncements whose
origins are many centuries old.[1] Their premises are creatures
of the desert, that silent presence, mute mentor and partner
of the church fathers and the obsessional mind, then and now.
In this context, too, Greek thinking comes to us in a special
guise.

For Paul, John, Anthony, Ambrose, Augustine, Tertullian,
Jerome, and others the desert and desertified landscapes sustained their vision of a split world. In its capacity for inspiring
images of opposition, the same environment that nurtured
the archaic agricultural theocracies celebrating the maternal
earth fostered an alienist view, a world-rejecting, abstract ascetic that would seep forward to link up with technology and
the neurotic presumptions and perceptions of our own time.

Thus the West rose distinctly in this oppositional mood,
scorning the native ceremonial life of all pagan earth worship-
ers and the power of chthonic forces that seemed nasty, de-
monic and pervasive. By the time Dionysian, Mesopotamian,
and Egyptian polytheisms had gone, the whole sensory world

would be wounded by "sacred discontent." The myth of the defeat of Tiamat by the sun god Marduk and the production of their son-messenger Mummu ("the Word") foreshadowed, even in Babylonian times, what was to come. The imperial Persian religion conceived the sun as the God of Truth, Ahura Mazda. Its major prophet, Zoroaster, was, says Joseph Campbell, the father of "Occidental ethical religiosity," a reformist spirit against the endless round of soil and seasons, a spurious victory over the body and the world by the illumination of righteousness and will. A synthesis of Mazda's principles with Christian gnosticism was made in the third century by Mani, from which an assortment of Manichaean guises would supply the Christian purists with countless expressions of the unresolved, divided nature of the world.

What they had renounced in the syncretic pagan societies were resolutions of such ambiguities. In the older, agri-high cultures, special ceremonies centering on the slaying of the bull were intended to renew and unite the world. "The function of these cults," says Campbell, "was to bring about a psychological transformation in the candidate for knowledge . . . in the realization that divinity inheres in, as well as transcends, every particle of the universe and all its beings; the realization that duality is secondary."[2]

It is not my contention that the desert environment gives rise to an ideology of opposition and duality, but that its perceived sensory qualities are compatible with such an idea, as though in a world with no dusk there were no mediating factor, no balance between relatedness and uniqueness, only definition by isolation. For Arabs before the horse was domesticated, for Navajos and Austrialian aborigines, and for individual minds bent on holism, the desert may have given its nuances and subtleties and its gradations between black and white. But for the fringe groups who were the Western cultural rudiments, it was not an affirmation of holism that they sought, but confirmation of a binary universe.

They found it not only in physical surroundings, but in the "Neolithic dialectic," the confrontation between herdsmen and farmers. It was a conflict at two levels: one an intermittent dialogue between two economic components of the societies of the Levant; the other the seminal incursions of mounted pastoralists from the north, successively demolishing the theocracies of the soil (only to be absorbed by the earth-centered traditions of the conquered people and, in time, becoming farmers, themselves invaded by new hordes from the north). Such Semitic desert nomads invaded and ruled Sumer nearly four thousand years ago; the Hurrians from the Caucasus, led by aristocratic Indo-Aryan chariot-fighters; warrior-herding Hittites, coming into Turkey; and the Kassites, who worshipped the sun and wind, are but a few. Similar invasions and confrontations also mark Greek history, where a Homeric Bronze Age culture with rapturous group rites was subordinated to Olympian rationalism, skepticism, and humanistic self-knowledge. The Mycenaeans, absorbed by the Minoan megaron culture after 1600 B.C., had themselves arrived from the north and were in turn overrun by Achaeans, allies of the Hittites, after 1300 B.C. and, a century later, by the pastoral warrior Dorians. All of which is to say that the background of both classical Greece and the Jewish Bible lands, of Zeus and of Yahweh, was a turmoil of armed mounted invaders from the north and east.

Joseph Campbell sees this transition from a farming to a pastoral ethos in Greece as the brink "of the most decisively productive century for the maturation of man's mind in the history of the world . . . the leap from the dark age of Homer's barbaric warrior kings to the day of luminous Athens . . . comparable to the passage without transition from boyhood dream (life mythologically compelled) to a self-governed young manhood . . . a self-responsible intelligence, released from both 'I want' and 'Thou shalt,' rationally regarding and responsibly judging the world of empirical facts, with the final aim not of serving gods but of developing and maturing man."[3]

Any number of other authors place a radical transformation of "human consciousness" in the same frame.[4] But what of "young manhood" achieved "without transition"? Is *mythos* really more immature than *logos*? Is there not some doubt that a rationally ordered system, regardless of how supremely logical, a dialectic of proofs and counterproofs, is the end of wisdom? Yet the pursuit of truth as discourse and empiricism seems normal to us, its inheritors. In Greece, the Ionian philosophers pursuing what was *true*, instead of what was *good*, won out, separating mind from matter, subject from object, form from substance; these conflicting entities, suggests Robert Persig, became the dynamic of the pseudomyth, history. The Sophists, seeking an organismic relativity of truth to thought, lost. Persig speaks of "the unbelievable magnitude of what man, when he gained power to understand and rule the world in terms of dialectic truths, had lost. He had built empires of scientific capability to manipulate the phenomena of nature into enormous manifestations of his own dreams of power and wealth—but for this he had exchanged an empire of understanding of equal magnitude: an understanding of what it is to be a part of the world, and not an enemy of it."[5]

Greek abstract thought sacrificed a mediating factor that Persig calls "quality." It is not, he says, that Greek ideas simply lead to rationality, to technology, and to destructiveness, but that some qualifying act or principle was sacrificed. Maybe it was lost in that "passage without transition" of Campbell's, an unforseen effect of Greek demythologizing on the initiation rituals and formalities that are central to the psychological transformation of the adolescent.

The Greeks' failure in their own time to become master technologists has been attributed to their fear of the "uncanny" aspect of the machine.[6] Uncanny means "mysteriously threatening," the terror experienced by psychopaths when confronted by an analogical image, such as caricature in art. A normal child assumes that all things that move, such as clouds, are alive and finds pictures of terrible monsters frightening. Normally the child grows out of that confusion as he develops the capacity to separate on the basis of an analogy, recognizing separate though common elements in different things. Such is metaphor, that mental miracle connecting myth to reality and discovering sacred significance in nature.

In other ways, also, the "maturity" of Periclean Greece seems typical of an immature personality. Of the Platonic ideal of neuter human relationships and pederasty linked to pedagogy, Campbell exclaims, "Everything that we read of it has a wonderful adolescent atmosphere of opalescent, timeless skies—untouched by the vulgar seriousness of a heterosexual commitment to mere life."[7]

In most of the myths of creation of an androgynous ancestor, there is a paradisical sexlessness or infantile autosexuality that is unmistakably puerile. Like all ideals of unity and fantasies of merger, it can be mistakenly viewed as the end of wisdom because it is associated with that universal mnemonic of embryonic peace before the trials of differentiation.

The Greek ideals of youthfulness and intellectual skepticism are celebrated roots of Western consciousness, but their price is high. The destruction of living myth was undertaken in Hellenistic times with the best intentions. It was accompanied by disillusion and anxiety, an angst familiar to our own times. There was what Lucretius called a lot of "bored rushing around," terrible fears alternating with apathy. He and Epicurus believed that the solution was a rational understanding of the world. But the new logic could not provide a world of purpose, lively with spiritual activity, its ceremonial celebrations deserving of deep fidelity; it was not an alternative to a mythic, ritual foundation for passage-making in the life stages of the individual.[8]

With the translation of the Old Testament from Latin to

Greek to create the Septuagint Bible and the interaction of Jewish and Greek cultures beginning in the third century B.C., two roots of the modern West were joined, sharing goals of spiritual and intellectual abstraction and asceticism.

The fanatic third- and fourth-century spokesmen for Christianity were among its most psychologically and ecologically destructive representatives, just as the New Testament was, from this standpoint, a purer formulation of otherworldliness. By omitting the metaphors and celebrations of the sacredness of the earth that had found their way into the Old Testament with a Canaanite earthiness, the New Testament became one of the world's most antiorganic and antisensuous masterpieces of abstract ideology, flecked with raw, ragtag bits of obscure patriarchal genealogy and fixation on vengeance and tribal war.

To their credit, the Christians themselves, especially in Europe, lived richer and fuller lives than the model proclaimed by that document of ultimate dissociation. For more than a thousand years they forced the austere Church to progressively back off, incorporate heathen celebrations and pagan rituals, wink its eye at festivals of the crops and seasons, and enlarge its tolerance for nonhumans and non-Christians —in short, to assume the posture of a kind of wisdom beyond its infantile hatreds, juvenile loyalties, and adolescent vaporizings. Even pessimistic, monkish, antilife prelates, like Pope Gregory I in the sixth century, were intimidated by indigenous folklore. It was as though the ontogeny of every individual coalesced in a transpersonal urge to seek the return of myth (however dressed in Christianized costumes), images and art, the omens and auguries of the natural world, and the psychic nourishment of initiation ceremony.[9]

This drift of orthodoxy toward sanity had two great culminations, one in twelfth-century art, naturalism, architecture, poetry, song, and love and the other in the nonreductionist, pre-Baconian sciences of biology and geology of the sixteenth century.[10] The glory of the twelfth and thirteenth centuries was a culmination as much as a beginning. Love of the natural world in the vision of Francis of Assisi, the diffusing energies of courtly love along with the recovery of the feminine, the ecstatic use of natural images as language in manuscript illustration, calendar and herbal art, the narratives of Reynard and the *Roman de la Rose,* and the animal observations of Albertus and Frederick II, along with the sculpturing of living forms in the cathedral architecture testify to a riddling of Christian asceticism with a Germanic sense of being. One would hardly guess from the Dantean macro-micro cosmos, crammed with meaning and movement, that such a "Christian" theme could have sprung from the alienist Hebrew prophets, Jewish monotheism, or Christian duality. Dante's zoo of angels and demons was a rich polytheism, invoking the medieval recovery of the spirituality of the stars, the clairvoyant effects of speech and thought, the principle of plenitude (the physical realization of all possibility), astrological medicine, the calendar, life and intelligence in all things, and above all the participatory role of men: these evoked a cybernetic finite world in which every thing and every event had some sacred—or diabolical—connection.

The medieval attitude, says Lewis, was not just philosophical, but had its practical side too. Men had more experience with and interest in animals: "The percentage of the population who knew a great deal about certain animals must have been far larger in medieval than in modern England. It could not have been otherwise in a society where everyone who could be was a horseman, hunter, and hawker, and everyone else a trapper, fisher, cowman, sheepherd, swineherd, goosegirl, henwife, or beekeeper."[11] The core of this medieval feeling was not a theory, but a way of experiencing. "To be intensely aware of participation is, for man, to feel the centre of energy in himself identified with the energy of which external nature is the image," writes Barfield.[12] It was a world in which every word, action, and thought had some impact on the world and in which every falling leaf or calling bird was a message to man.

Since time immemorial this mode of connectedness has been symbolized as intercourse, celebrated in phallic cults or in fertility goddesses—just those figures from which Jews and Aristotelian Christian drew back.[13] Lewis's *The Discarded Image* is so poetic on medieval man's at-homeness in the world that one wonders that his version of Medieval Christianity is the same religion of Pope Innocent III's *Contemptus Mundi* in the tenth century or of St. Anselm's sour denunciation of all sensuousness in the twelfth. Although aware of the traditional "mystical, ascetic, world-renouncing theology of neo-Platonism," Lewis waxes enthusiastic for the "kindly encycling" (gravity) holding the great primum mobile together, full of "sympathies" and "striving" rather than manipulation or regulation of natural laws, conveying the idea that it is the loss of Christian feeling that is at the root of modern anomie and estrangement.

It is odd that those who have defended Christianity against the charge that its attitudes contribute to the denudation of the planet and catastrophic extirpation of animals do not celebrate this Dantean cosmos, whose lively spiritual diversity is rather like an ecosystem, with its precise niches and unifying flow of energy.[14]

Reference to the rejection of the organic imagery of the underbelly of thought brings us closer to the Protestant puritanic subject of this essay. Signs of duality so accessible to the eye in the desert are not so obvious where soil blankets the earth, trees interdigitate with the sky and lace the horizon, shadows are penumbral, and plants everywhere are a lively skin over the rock bones beneath. In Celtic Europe, philosophies of dichotomy needed other cadences to make converts among peasants and villagers. In the great forests of primeval France and Germany, richer in birds and animals than the Levant had been for thousands of years, what could the biblical mind do with all this animation, the vast mulch of creatures, growth, and decay? It found the objective realization of a philosophy in the fearful potential of organic fructification and the muckiness of wet decay, as opposed to the order of the farm or of the city itself. The distinction between wilderness (as desert) and paradise had been a useful tool in the literal-minded opposition of barrenness and fruition, hence punishment and reward. But the northern virgin forest and the Garden of Eden have a kind of synonymy that confuses such easy juvenile imagery.

Postglacial Europe, even the periglacial Mediterranean shores, was a swampy place. The most fertile soils were often those, from an agricultural and medical point of view, most in need of drainage. The reclamation of wetlands played an enormous role in the civilized history of the continent and an equal role, I believe, in the psychohistory of those for whom the symbols of a new duality were being shaped. There is an undeniable unconscious substrate in which this muckiness is also the landscape of human origin. The stork who delivers babies in the folktale can do so because he is a long-legged wader who is seen plucking wet wriggling forms from the swamps. Falsely purified by our ignorance of his true habits, he is imagined coming from the sky with his human bundle, but in reality he is a connection to the great genetrix, the Mother Earth. Disgust with the site of human genesis was not new to Christianity, but its homology in wet wild lands provided the puritanical reformers, who protested against the acquiescence of the orthodox Church to worldly numina, a terrestrial expression of that which they had always feared most: their own bodies.

For the Christian puritans of the sixteenth and later centuries, the city had become what the desert was to the Hebrew prophets and the Christian puritans of Roman times: an arid pavement in which space was defined by human logic derived from celestial observation, a cultural nowhere that allowed the etherialized believers to disengage from paths across the earth and the cults of the soil. In the Near East, the feminine epiphany was the terrain of the cradling lap of the goddess, centered on sacred springs and rivers, set off and surrounded by the drier uplands with their pastoral, patriarchal associations. But in Europe she was potentially everywhere in her leafy tunic and fecund wetness—except the city.[15]

This Protestant detachment was parallel to the contemporary arts of portrait and landscape painting. The subjective pretense of "being there" was achieved by the mathematical distancing in a measurable space. A moment in time and point in distance needed for scrutiny and analysis created the conscious spectator, separated from the object viewed.[16] This fracturing of experience was everywhere. Similar discontinuities separating observer from outer space arose in the Copernican discovery of the astronomical universe. A microscopic world and a paleontological distancing gained something at the cost of a grievous sense of loss. Recovery of this lost something—nature, innocence, participation—requires, psychologically, returning to a beginning. That, in turn, requires the destruction of an unsatisfactory world, producing a kind of ruin iconography. The seventeenth-century geological explanation of the existence of mountains was in terms of natural ruins, reflecting the taste for catastrophe and destruction linked to a felt need for rejuvenation and the recovery of paradise. All paradises, says Eliade, reveal a yen for reformist demolition.

Other art of the time exhibited still other Protestant concerns. The backgrounds of German paradisical landscape paintings of meadows with crumbling arches, eroding caves, and lumpy hillocks are unmistakable analogies of the body, perceptual instruments evoking the torso as a spoiled garden. Hieronymus Bosch, says Norman Brown, painted Luther's obsession with corruption, a kind of anality as landscape. The rottenness of inner and outer nature in all its sensory aspects is represented.

This is the basis of that dark side of the celebrated "inwardness" of the Occidentals, the guilt and self-analysis to which modern Westerners are heir, and the inevitable emergence of a physical satanic reality over against the search for the recovery of a pure state. The Protestants emphasized not only disgust and horror and fascination with bowels and genitals, but with death and the curse on the whole realm of the organic—on life itself.

Avalanches of psychological, clinical, and analytic therapy have shown that being out of touch with the body is the basic schizoid position.[17] It connects at one end with the nature of the first fourteen years and on the other with philosophy and theology, however crudely or archetypically expressed in ordinary folkways or elegantly dressed out by pedants. It governs the effect of the senses and is transferred to outer reality. It is inseparable from the species-wide concern with pollution, with that attention to what is clean and what is unclean, driven inward so implacably and with such regressive intensity that it colors all outer action. In the substitution of nature for the body, the individual and culture reveal an inadequate differentiation and the lack of metaphorical links that make a mature sense of likeness-in-unlikeness possible. The earth/body analogy, the vision of nature-as-physiology, of human kinship as a kind of ecological system, the projections of sexual dimorphism on the nonhuman world—all such analogies are fundamental to healthy human consciousness.

For the infant and child there are no analogies. The primary experience is that of unity and symbiosis. Otherness is incorporated. Analogy exists only with reference to location. The experience of one's own body is at first the only keyboard there is, and external nature, as it is experienced bit by bit, is transposed by our perception as variations on known themes.[18] Normal development enables the individual to make progressively better distinctions between his own mother and the Mother Earth, while at the same time expanding the symbols that enable him to retain his intuition of common underlying structure. He masters all kinds of bridges that eventually turn the black-and-white world of the infant's good-or-bad mother into a plural, qualified world.

How we feel about our bodies is, in this way, related to how we use language and how we think and feel about a great variety of other things. And that how is not philosophical at all, but a physical and psychological development. In compliance with it, we invent a logic and find suitable ideas to fit our feelings. Even the moderate and genteel society of modern secular American-Europeans is committed to sanitizing the world by the collusion of technology and puritanism. The extirpation of nonhuman life everywhere touched by Western economics is the distant voice of puritan self-contempt and devil hunting.[19]

The root of this estrangement from the self is a kind of "unity pathology,"—from the mother.[20] In its most emphatic pastoral and patriarchal expressions—in the desert fathers of the Jews and then the Christians, and finally in the Protestants in all their secular forms—there is a deep yearning to be the male guide, whose task is to energize the child's shift from one matrix to the next. But in the puritan West one is led in this to reject rather than expand the bodily and maternal matrices. The ideology hovers over this obstacle, stranding the individual in his misguided division of loyalties, in which he repudiates the only models there are of a coherent and

meaningful world: his own body, his mother, and the landscape of his childhood.

The abuse of the body, like the abuse of the natural world,
is the traditional puritan response. But the attempt to humili-
ate and master leads to preoccupation. That is the snare the
puritan sets for himself; death, birth, sex, excretion, secre-
tion, digestion, and the kinesthetics of metabolism become
the foreground on which he wrestles with the devil. Just as a
god stooped to be incarnated in his religion, his body
becomes a lower self in his psychology. Behind the proud
self-consciousness and conscience of the puritan is the despair of his own organism, fear of that involuntary and unconscious aspect of the self inaccessible to control. Nothing so
clearly identifies the West as the distrust of the powers of the
earth, focused at last upon the undomesticatable wildness
within.

The most antiseptic and fire-purified earth is the desert.
So the Christians took it along everywhere. Introspection
turned the wetland of the natural self into a dry rectitude. One
scrutinized nature and one's own natural inclinations the way
the Hebrew fathers had scourged and cauterized chthonic
cosmologies and mythologies. The Christian reformists took
cues from the harsher aspects of both Testaments, adding a
severer sense of evil and putting individual choice in place of
the chosen people with a prudishness so thoroughgoing that
it would set the tone of middle-class decorum for centuries.[21]

The denigration of the body by puritanic thought looks
back to infantile doubts and fears about the body. Its im-
maturizing effect spreads to the feminine and to nature,
whose fortunes rise and fall in tandem, linked by metaphor
and symbol. They are alike in the mystery of their autonomous creativity, of growing instead of being shaped from the
outside, and the ways in which each represents the other in
the growth of consciousness. The emergence of a body per-

cept and the simultaneous fixation on the mother's face are keystones in the gestalt of a coherent world for the infant. It sheds its order onto the world at large. No adult ideology of nature as dirty is really convincing unless that primary experience was disabled and the first symbiosis blocked.[22]

The drama of adolescent theorizing, instruction, and initiation carries this broken pattern into his picture of creation. When adolescence is controlled by a dichotomizing cult, the temporarily reexperienced bad body, in the normal adolescent mood of renewed, infantile experience, can be made to seem diabolic. And so, too, can the whole realm of nature be grasped as flawed.

But their dualizing mode of thought prevents the purists from thoroughgoing hatred of the world. The fear and contempt for a "howling wilderness" is only one side of the Protestant experience in America. Its abyssal corruption is opposed by luminous freshness. In New England, John Davenport said of nature, "There is never a leaf in this Book, but hath something of God written legibly upon it, and many characters of his Divine power, wisdom, and goodness there engraven."[23]

For Jonathan Edwards, the earthly realm shadowed forth spiritual matters on every hand, and he responded rapturously. Historian Perry Miller has described this strain of eighteenth-century puritanism as pre-Wordsworthian or pre-Emersonian.[24] Quoting George Turnbull's "*External things are intended to be images of things spiritual, moral and divine,*" Edwards sought to make a "dictionary of divine discourse," to comprehend an inexpressible glory "in the dialect of created things." It seems contradictory that the dour Yankees could have been so quick to admire nature. How is it that their renewed patriarchy fostered what would become romanticism: interest in the landscape; a sensitivity to feminine style and mythology; and attention to the ambiguities of hidden, secret springs and meanings of life and the numinous aspects of the great round?

The answer lies in the schizoid nature of unity pathology, the infantilisms of separation anxiety and impaired identity processes. Their rationalization was largely in terms of paradise, a respectable religious theme connecting them to their Hebrew roots. The shift from disgust with the body to the imagery of America as paradise is just the sort of ambivalent behavior associated with a destabilized concept of the self. For years I puzzled over this ambiguity in American life: one society—the world's most ferocious destroyers and yet the most fanatic preservers of wilderness parks and endangered species. Neurotic love, says Jay Gonen, includes "an overwhelming desire to rescue the beloved." The two opposite positions are merely sides of the puritan passion, aspects of a double vision derived from early-life experiences and psychology and similar the world over to those of other patriarchal peoples.[25]

The vision of America as paradise is connected to a passion for the millennium, a nostalgia for the destructuring that must precede a transformation of the earth.[26] The new Adam would live, of course, in an untainted garden. In due course the Protestants would attempt to sterilize North America in a more severe manner than the compromising Catholics who had assimilated paganism and dealt with the land in Latin America.

In *Man in the Landscape* I examined the idea of paradise in the era of European exploration and colonialism. Bernard Smith, in his fine *European Vision and the South Pacific,* made much the same point: Westerners in unfamiliar environments, prompted by expectations of novelty and wealth, drew heavily on a long tradition of travel lore that was inseparable from a paradise mythology and which, by the eighteenth century, was available in pictorial form.[27] However, Smith and I

89

overemphasized an iconographic factor. The paradise theme in travel signifies a regressive state of mind. Europeans not only carried fantastic images to new lands, but were in touch with these fantasy worlds through the medium of their own early experience. It should not be surprising if their thought and behavior in many ways were immature.[28]

Mircea Eliade interprets the utopian dream and paradisical imagery of Protestant America as autistic adolescent psychopathology.[29] To borrow a phrase from process philosophy, the paradise ideal as the goal of social action and of political, religious, and ecological transformation, is "misplaced concreteness." The ancient worldwide shamanistic view of the Other World seldom confused it with This World, and access by an extraordinary spiritual act remained distinct. The medieval Christian spiritualizing of "desert" and "wilderness" and "paradise" as states of mind would seem to preserve the distinction, but such fine allegorizing and intellectualizing was just what the Protestant reformists sought to end. The literalizing impulse of the sixteenth century was one of those broad shifts in cultural style that show us the shared underpinnings of modern science and Christian fundamentalism, both riveted to a juvenile insistence on positivistic, utilitarian thought.

The universal yearning for paradise described by Eliade, the compendium of descriptions of the Other World by Howard Rollin Patch, and a vast anthropological/mythological literature attest to the idea of another world throughout mankind.[30] But the similarities can be misleading. Eckstein and Caruth see utopian thought as a means that "fulfills the psychic function of allowing the working through of a conflict in order to achieve a resolution" and the agency by which "the world of immediate impulse fulfillment must be renounced in favor of the world of reality in order to gain the capacity for postponement, delay and intermittent gratification which must be sought for and worked for. . . ."[31]

In other words, the collective dream of making a utopia forces the society to take account of reality in somewhat the same way the impossible fantasies of infancy allow the baby to tolerate its yearnings. The blissful bodily state dreamed by the infant and the idyllic natural world of the child, yearned for in nostalgia for sensory comfort by the adolescent, are not recoverable. What the adolescent should know is that these are aspects of experience, not places, and he is prepared to comprehend them as elements in the amazing myth of creation if he enters a maturing tuition and cosmocising initiation.

Deferring gratification is a juvenile achievement against infantile impatience, so Eckstein and Caruth may be right as far as they go. But the transformation of a (lost) paradise into a (future) utopia gains only three or four years in maturity. It is a common observation that the ideologies of progress spring from this redirection of forward yearning rather than backward repining, and indeed, one wonders whether the avidity for change and purchases of goods on credit in modern society says much for deferred gratification.[32]

Eliade tells of paradising as the key to Western sensibility, played out in the occupation of the North American continent. Destruction is its prelude. The orgies of spoiling, the messianic and apocalyptic atmosphere, the hatred of history and tradition are all familiar themes in American genesis, all typical of antinomian behavior, giving literal rather than ritual enactment of adolescence's end of childhood.

The contradiction within American Protestant culture—which continues today—is its emotional enthusiasm for the beauty of virgin scenery set against the materialist "ethic" expressed collectively as corporate arrogance in the destruction of soil, grass, water, and forests. But examination shows the contradiction to be superficial. The puritanical fear of pollution as seen in the messiness of the body and nature, as when John Mather observed that "we shall not heal the crooked perversity of our natures by learning about the creation," is cut from the same fabric as the puritanical urge to cleanse the stains.

Yet the wilderness does serve the individual as part of his epigenesis. An errantry is mediated by elders in a religious act that propels the candidate forward. The yearning for that vision-seeking may in part account for the success of the books by Carlos Castaneda, experiences not based on pictorial idealizing but on a profound transformation arising in confrontations in nature. It is clear, however, that the official American wildernesses, the national parks, were never understood by most Americans to be used that way. Otherwise those lands would not have been humanized, emphasizing scenery, science, standardized recreation, protectionism, and the use of machines in maintenance.

As the nation developed, the widespread personal search for nature surrendered itself to science and esthetics or was driven forward in the name of progress toward that paradise which first requires an inferno. The Protestants were both intellectual and romantic, pietistic and evangelical. Among the latter, the fundamentalists have been working their way back to Calvin, the desert fathers, and the prophets ever since, abetted by the fact that the psychological disturbances generated by the infantilisms of the self and body could, with greater freedom than in Europe, be expressed as action in the landscape.

5

The Mechanists

—

ITIS ODD, after seventy centuries of city life, that we continue to be uneasy about it and uncertain as to what is wrong. The situation is like those psychological illnesses in which the patient shows a devilish capacity to obscure the real problem from himself. A demon seems to make false leads, so that deliverance requires more of the same, confusing problem and symptom. It is as though traffic, smog, disease, violence, crime, uncaring strangers, dirt, drug addiction, and unemployment collectively provide distraction from something that perhaps cannot be dealt with.

The city's central role in harm to world biomes, especially when dressed as success rather than failure, surely has more subtle roots than bad strategy or inept philosophy. Can we make a radical leap beyond explanations citing unjust laws, torpid administration, miseducation or graft?

Let us suppose, with some evidence, that the city is typically a sink of psychological problems. In the individual these are partly caused by city life, but in the longer view they cause the city. Where can the cycle be broken, and what are its processes? To gain a start, the psychological dimension may be characterized as a disease of attention—that is, the focused operations of human consciousness between directed sensory experience and memory, between the perception of phenomena and their formulation. This area of individual consciousness mediating experience and theory develops from habits of early life, linked to the start of speech in the infant, to personal identity formation patterned by child-rearing customs and adult assumptions.

The evidence is good that our fellow creatures individually and collectively show distorted behavior when their numbers go beyond a norm for the species. The symptoms of overcrowding include almost every organic and social dysfunction. Rats and rabbits congregate in dense immobile clusters or "behavioral sinks."[1] Horses and mice abort. Fish show increased homosexuality. In general, all share physiological abnormalities and impaired reproductive lives. Among primates, the group or noyau (the society of balanced recrimination, or brotherhood of tempered conflict) degenerates into chaos, with killing, maiming, tyranny, attacks on females and young, and heavy stress in the whole group.[2]

In higher animals of many kinds, including man, the depletion of physical resources may not begin to signal "too many" until long after psychological damage has begun. By the time the subsistence base of physical resources begins to show signs of excessive withdrawals, some behavioral processes may be so distorted that the group lacks the flexibility to make an adjustment. Of course, the topic of human numbers is confusing because there is no agreement as to what "too many" means. Death from famine in Bangladesh or Biafra or Cambodia may be "caused" by too many people or, according to a different perspective, by too little food—which results from poor strains of seed, lack of transportation, bad weather, government policy, or former colonialism. As Garrett Hardin says, ironically, "Nobody ever dies of overpopulation."[3]

Perhaps one of the density distortions in human psychology is a kind of desperate togetherness. Urbanization affects human biology in ways for which the organism was not prepared by evolution.[4] The logic of this peculiar massing is that

94

there is no limit to human numbers, short of space itself. Low or declining numbers become a kind of fearful specter. The writers of history, for example, revel in the growth of human numbers and tremble at their decline.

Bang, whang, whang, goes the drum, *tootle-te-tootle* the fife.
Oh, a day in the city-square, there is no such pleasure in life![5]

So sang Robert Browning, and he is not disproved by modern psychology or anthropology, which show that man is "naturally" a lover of high-contact, high-proximity living. One study from the Kalahari Desert of Africa observes that the !Kung bushmen, though living in small groups in vast savannas, like to sit touching each other around their fires at night and build their huts close together: Eureka! They like crowding![6] Another concludes that the crime and violence of cities cannot be correlated with density as measured by people per square mile, but must be examined as people per block, apartment buildings per block, number of apartments per building, number of rooms per apartment, or number of people per room.[7] Still another argues that it is not high density itself that causes city miseries but the *effects* of density.[8] (No, Inspector, the man was not killed by a murderer at all, but by a bullet entering his brain.)

Among people, the effects of stress and anxiety associated with the conditions of urban life have manifold symptoms, including virtually every physical complaint and emotional twitch, sexual deviation, and chaotic child rearing. The "tendency to paranoia," a pervasive feeling of fear, provokes the individual into spurious explanations with perceptual and ideological consequences.[9] Given such parents and adult mentors, the child exposed to the city effect is vulnerable to distortions of those episodes of conceptual order making that shape the individual in the first dozen years of life.

Embryology tells us that growth is a tightly latticed regimen. Within it, the earlier a defect occurs, the more general and irreparable its effect. Damage to a single cell may do little harm to a four-month-old embryo, whereas in the one-month-old embryo it could lead to severe anomaly by affecting all the thousands of cells descending from the one damaged. A good pathologist can tell the age within days at which a fetus was injured by looking at the adult many years later.

This principle also extends to the brain and therefore the fine-tuning of the mind. The psyche has its own phases and is more vulnerable in the early months of life. Like the muscles of an arm, which require use to begin on schedule and continue or they wither, perceptual and sensory needs are locked into a calendar in which distortions and the want of use can have lasting effects.[10]

Many psychologists do not concur in the picture of irreversibility suggested above. The field of developmental psychology is a widely recognized and active discipline. Large amounts of data exist, and yet the results generally seem abysmally lacking in wisdom for living on a planet, in a natural world, and in guidance for being an intelligent land animal— primate or mammal—or for nurturing the developing mind as one species among many. My impression is that, as in other social sciences, there is a majority denial of norms for the human environment. A typical textbook does not deal with the nonhuman living world at all, yet G. Stanley Hall, of an earlier (and perhaps wiser) generation, wrote:

City life favors knowledge of mankind, physics, and perhaps chemistry, but so removes the child from the heavens and animate nature that it is pathetic to see how unknown and merely bookish knowledge of them becomes to the town-bred child. Biology, that has given us evolution, is perhaps farthest from recognizing the necessity of developing a genetic pedagogy that shall very slowly pass over to the adult logical stage which cross-sections it only when it has completed its own. How undeveloped the development theory still is is here seen in the fact that it has not yet drawn its own obvious but momentous lesson for education where it has its most fruitful field of application. When this science knows life histories as well as it does morphology it will have the material with which to begin aright. We no longer deform the child's body, and have in more and more ways recognized its rights, but we still arrest and even mutilate the soul of adolescence by prematurely forcing it into the mental mold of grown-ups. Instead of the ideal of knowing or doing one thing minutely well, like the ant, bee, or wasp, we should construct, even if at certain points it be done tentatively and out of glimpses, *aperçus,* hints, a true universe, and pass from the whole to parts and not *vice versa.* Love of nature always burgeons in the soul of youth, but its half-grown buds are picked open or stunted, and disenchantment too often leaves the soul only a few mouthfuls of wretched desiccated phrases, as meager and inadequate as those of poetry in a conventional age that has drifted far from her. . . .

The sentiments on which the highest religion rests are best trained in children on the noblest objects of nature. Natural theology once had, and is destined in new forms to have again, a great role in the intellectual side of religious training. So, too, in many summer meetings, twilight services on hills or exposed to vesper influences, perhaps out-of-doors, are found to have wondrous reenforcements. Worship on a hill or mountain, at the shore, out at sea, under towering trees, or in solemn forests or flowery gardens, amidst harvest scenes, in moonlight, at midnight, at dawn, in view of the full moon, with the noises of the wind or streams, the hum of insects, the songs of birds, or in pastoral scenes, is purer and more exalting for these pagan influences set to the music of nature from which they all took their origin, than it can ever be in stuffy churches on noisy city streets upon the dull or familiar words of litany, sermon, or Scripture. Here, again, so-called "progress" has broken too completely with the past and forgotten the psychogenesis of religion, which has thus grown anemic, superficial, and formal. It is the old error of amputating the tadpole's tail rather than letting it be absorbed to develop the legs that make a higher life on land possible.[11]

In the crisis of urban/industrial life, the issue of genetically programmed development and the inherent needs of the infant for certain aspects of the external, nonhuman world is most acute. In this framework we can be more precise about what the growing mind misses and what connection there might be between the absence of natural things and the distortions of human behavior that engulf the modern city like an epidemic.

An outer and an inner natural history are intertwined. Stanley Milgram, writing of the tuning down of the psyche as an act of self-protection—and therefore noninvolvement—explains it as a "natural" means of coping with a heavy human-contact burden. Human nature is limited in its capacity to respond hospitably to strangers and has an inbuilt, predictable shutting-down response to high human density.[12]

But Milgram's argument does not go far enough. It does not cover an outer domain of impoverishment in the city that has helped create the predisposition to perceive people as alien. All children experience the world as a training ground for the encounter with otherness. That ground is not the arena of human faces but whole animals. Nonhuman life is the real system that the child spontaneously seeks and internalizes, matching its salient features with his own inner diversity. He seeks these correspondences, implicit in language, games, and the tales told by his caretakers. A metaphor is to be invoked later in his life, when he awakens to the richness of the Other in himself. After his twelveth year, he begins to evoke, as though caricaturing, one or another of these elements of himself. His shared humanity is a shared foxiness, frogness, or owlness.

The city contains a minimal nonhuman fauna. Adequate otherness is seldom encountered. A self does not come together that can deal with its own strangeness, much less the aberrant fauna and its stone habitat. City-bred mothers are incompetent models of the metaphor, and fathers are travesties of its administration. The world to the child—and adult—is grotesquely, not familiarly, Other.

In this scenario, childrearing is not simply the victim of the urban debacle, but the causal root of the adult's inability to make the city any different. Charity and kindness in such a place become the province of impersonal agencies.

The following observations are elements of the malaise of modern loneliness and alienation as an urban affliction:

Helplessness. Human anxiety begins here, said Sigmund Freud. Infantile fantasies of power are, he said, compensations for the baby's physical incapacity to do anything for itself and for the stress of occasional loneliness, hunger, and inner and outer discomfort. To be helpless is, to the modern mind, the worst of all fates. Savages, says Eric Hoffer, are subject to the whims of nature. The ideology of progress is mainly one of increasing our domination over nature.[13] The culture is saturated with the necessity of increasing, and the fear of losing, control. The quest for power, says Karen Horney, is the trait of our time.[14] The idea is desperately in the air—control of weight, smoking, drinking, violence, inflation, the economy, communism, imperialism, world markets. . . . But the idea of control is merely the last act, the rationalized and articulated expression of a widely shared, frighteningly acute sense of need. The dream of omnipotence is an infantile dream that should diminish, rather than grow, with personal maturity. Unchecked, says Anthony Storr, it becomes an obsession, leading on to an overpolarized world view in which everything is either good or bad.[15] According to Louis J. Halle, such a view is the womb of all ideology of "us against them."[16]

Among plants and animals, as seen by the child and perceived through tales told and mimicked in game and play, there are thousands of metaphors of parts of himself. In each episode the rest are the Other. In the drama of nonhuman life, helplessness is never total, for the eaten is also the eater. How can this be, you might ask—how can he who is destroyed then become the destroyer? The answer is that perceptually a species can seem to be an individual. The blue jay may be eaten today by a hawk, but tomorrow he is seen again, eating a beetle. It is not a matter of compromise, nor of wins weighed against losses, but a different kind of structure from the either/or form of ideology. To internalize the blue jay is to grow out of the fantasy of omnipotence as the cure for helplessness.

To an infant girl, the world is both marvelous and terrible. But as mother she will shed this ambiguity if she herself learned the lesson of the blue jay as a child. If not, and she is split between being guiltily evil and arrogantly divine, how can her child learn otherwise? How can she know where and how the child is to learn the totemic secret of animal purpose? Her intuition that the natural world is a treasury of avatars invites all sorts of frauds and distortions, and her own aching sense of helplessness in mass society is accompanied by her grieving for something lost.

Helplessness is the disease of powerlessness in a frightening world of vague and contending forces. It is a world where one's own security is perceived as a lifelong struggle against others for status and domination. Nature, in this thwarted and anguished image, has lost its magical capacity to reveal that an ultimate symbiosis holds the universe together. Failing to serve one purpose, nature can serve another. It becomes the enemy for those who cannot face their own unconscious assumption that all other people are hostile.

Artifactual reality. Does the world grow or is it made? Philosophically it is not difficult to show that the question is somewhat trivial because beneath the surface of things the distinction fades. But there is a time in the life of each individual when the separation and grouping of things is the paramount intellectual activity. This name-tagging, category making is a species trait, but the categories themselves tend to be somewhat arbitrary. For example, a basic scheme may place all things as either "of the earth" or "of the water," or it may separate them as "spiritual" and "natural." Claude Levi-Strauss believes the separation of things into "cultural" and "natural" to be a fundamental and universal human activity. Perhaps a cultural form of this is the classification of "living" versus "nonliving," but not all peoples believe the nonliving to be without some inner life or spiritual autonomy. It is the distinction of the desert civilizations and especially of the scientific West to make the absolute division between what is made and what grows, though the niggling truce between science and Christianity allows for God to have made the first generation of living things.

The truism that man has created God in his own image can take evidence from the increasing importance of the creator-as-maker as historical man surrounded himself with a world he made. We may ask, going back beyond history, what the effects are, on a thinking being who evolved in a world where almost everything glimmered with life, of being thrust abruptly (in an evolutionary or geological sense) into a man-made world where things are presumed to be dead clay, without inner fire. The question has been asked before, but mistakenly addressed to adult reality, as though, for the individual, philosophy came before perception.

The made world of modern man is related to the child in somewhat the same way that the hospital is to the infant. Infants in understaffed orphanages suffer profound psychological deformity for lack of the touch of living flesh: the nonmothering results in retarded development or even death. Normal mothering does not simply produce survival or an enlargement of the infant's strength and powers; it moves the infant to a new plateau. The satisfactory culmination in the first three years of a good symbiosis with the mother endows the child with the emotional and intellectual potential for entering into a new set of relationships with a wider structure, social and ecological. At about age three the child goes out into the world. His nine-year mission is to build confidently from his good-mother symbiosis a lively relationship with a new and even more complex earth player, to slowly master new patterns of nonhuman life that will, in time, serve his identity shaping when he enters the adult social world as an adolescent.[17]

And what difference can it make if those nine years are played out in a fabricated environment? The absence of numerous nonhuman lives, a variegated plant-studded soil, the nearness of storms, wind, the odors of plants, the fantastic variety of insect forms, the surprise of springs, the mystery of life hidden in water, and the round of seasons and migrations —how does the lack of these really hurt the child?

First, life in a made world slowly builds in the child the feeling that nonlivingness is the normal state of things. Existence is shaped from the outside or put together. Eventually he will conclude that there is no intrinsic unfolding, no unique, inner life at all, only substance that, being manipulated, gives the illusion of spontaneity.[18]

Second, when he goes back into society after adolescence, having missed the initiation into the world of final mysteries and its poetry, he will believe either that (a) all life, including people, is, in fact, machines (I suspect this idea will prevail if his original mother has been inadequate) or (b) the only truly living things are people; this opens the door for all the dichotomies that separate the human from the nonhuman on the basis of soul, spirit, mind, history, culture, speech, rights, right to existence, and so on.

Third, he becomes either a spectator or an exploiter. The world may be interesting and useful or dull and useless, but it is not one that feels or thinks or communicates, that has special messages for him, or that has independent purposes

of its own. The world's inability to feel is his own mechanical
response projected upon it. He is like the infant whose emotions are crippled because he was suspended too long in an
inert world.

The philosophical consequences of this artifactual perspective dominate the history of Western mind: God the *maker*
who works from the outside rather than as an indwelling
spirit; the Greek atomists and their intellectual reductionist
descendents; the machine paradigm of the universe, from
Galileo to Buckminster Fuller, including the model of the
human body as machine from Vesalius to the men in space;
and, finally, relativistic thought from self-help psychology to
the existentialism of absurdity, which concludes that the only
reality is whatever you make of it, including the self.[19]

But it is not the philosophy as such that counts. It is how
our daily lives are lived. We continually take the world into
ourselves as the means of self-understanding. If we treat our
food as chemicals, it ceases to nourish and begins to poison
us. If we treat living things as chemical-physical compounds,
the message nutrient that they furnish to the mind is "You are
only an accumulation of compounds—behave accordingly."
If we replace the soft earth with pavement, we will learn in our
child's heart that the planet is a desert and a dead rock.[20]

Chaos. One of the threads that connects otherwise diverse
theories and studies of child development is the common
observation that the task of youth is to discover structure in
the world: meaningful constancy, predictable patterns, regularity, rhythm, familiar systems, stable relations. The child
wants to find a coherent world that remains true during his
own changes.[21] Progress and civilization seem to bring
"order" out of the wilderness. We have all seen the geometry
of the humanized world from the air, a striking contrast to the
raw tumult of the mountain wilderness. The city seems to
epitomize this symmetry-making of the human will.

And yet it is not so—and it is on this point more than any other that ecological insight conflicts with modern thought. Urban civilization delivers a topographical simulacrum of order to the perceiving child as a substitute for a middle ground of tangible, durable patterns that are truly complex and, in a special way, nonhuman. The streets of the medieval city retained much that fit the child's needs: animals on foot; place defined by uniqueness; the visible flow of water, food, and waste; human activity in religious and craft neighborhoods. The regular patterns of the modern geometrical or "cartographic" city do not create order, but repetition. Their inhuman scale is still not nonhuman. The child is not ready for the order implicit in the centralization of power and the mechanization of life that are indicated by that scale.

The adult can get along well enough, for much of the structure in his life can be abstract. Yet his earlier yearning for good spatial orientation, for neighborhood and creaturely mystery he remembers. He wants them for his own children. His exploration of those feelings, if undertaken by reading, is perverted by the nature of literature itself—we are back to kerygma, the preaching, proclaiming, prophesying mode in which the Hebrew inventors of literature denounced the myth-oriented cities of their time. Literature tells us that this yearning is only fantasy and nostalgia for something that "never" existed. It tells us to put no trust in our grieving for place, nature, continuity with the earth, or the significance of the seasons. Only the illiterate go on dumbly loyal to a lost reality, for the educated know that it is merely an infantile dream and that the true function of art is to create a luscious disorder.

The city child is asked, in effect, to proceed directly from his symbiosis with his mother to a mastery of social relations. He is to skip the genetic interlude in this task, in which he indulges for eight or ten years in nature, and go directly to the real job of life. During this time his frustration and inarticulate desire will be anesthetized by portrayals of the nonhuman as entertainment, not in the oral traditions of poetry, for that is a complement rather than a substitute for his submersion in otherness, but in an array of images—toys, pictures, zoos and gardens, decorations, Disney films, motifs and designs—a stew of nature so arbitrarily presented that the results of his years of trying to fix it in his heart will only lead to despair.[22] No wonder the child of thirteen years turns with such keen interest to machines. Man-portrayed nature has proved incoherent.

By my concentration on the child's need for nonhuman nature I do not mean to imply that the child from three to twelve is not also busy becoming a social being. His growth in relation to siblings, peers, parents, and others is widely studied and well known. What is less clear is the way in which this socialization is related to his experience with the nonhuman, the otherness that catalyzes his social relationships and prepares him for adolescent fixation on communal and religious ideals. I suspect, for example, that the substitution of animal toys and pictures as a kind of appeasement damages the individual's *social* relations, that it convinces him at some deep level that the given state of man is without pattern or purpose, that men have unlimited capacity to fabricate things, or that social organization is not a realization of human potential, but the outfall from belief, that is, the by-product of ideology.

For such an individual, the nonhuman elements of the self must be regarded with suspicion. One's bowels, like snakes or grasshoppers, must be regulated. One must take charge of the inner and outer world, either as a tyrant and spoiler or as God's steward. The symbolic use of nature for conceptualizing human affairs vanishes, except in trite parables. Arbitrary meaning, after all, is no meaning at all.

For such individuals, chaos becomes essential to the rage for order. Making a new order destroys a previous one, however provisional. George Steiner speaks of modern society's "nostalgia for disaster," "the perpetuity of crisis," "burning of the garden," "the dreams of ruins," our combining the "Judaic summons to perfection" with our "loathing of an impossible goal."[23] I take Steiner's meaning in ways that he may not have intended, for he describes with terrifying lucidity that will to devastation by those who are vexed over the imperfections of society, but whose real anger is resentment of being crippled—or, more accurately, a wrath evoked by the socially crippling deprivation of an orderly universe during the only years when that order can be internalized.

No wonder that, for us, the civilized landscape as seen from an aircraft looks more organized than the wilderness. Its blocks and circles and bold outlines are like child's blocks. The sense of oneself in space is a mature right-brain phenomenon. This ranges from the movements of the body in dance to geographic consciousness. The schizoid's confusion about where he is at any moment finds its analogy (or an expression?) in the urban loss of orientation by sun, stars, wind, terrain, or vegetational clues. Location given only by grid coordinates, as in the names of the nearest street junctions, would be intolerable to hunter-foragers. The antecedent of this spatial confusion is the desert, where the land all looked alike and one's place became a matter of tribal affiliation and ideology. Indeed, each of the great episodes with which this book deals has made its contribution to this disease of dislocation.[24]

What is said above may appear inconsistent with the psychological concept of environmental independence as a measure of maturity in the child. One psychological test measures the subject's ability to maintain verticality despite visual clues. The child dependent on such clues is said to perceive globally and to be more infantile than one who knows up from down regardless of sensory tricks. But the contradiction is only superficial. A mature sense of identity does not rely on such orientation at any given moment, but is the outcome of developmental processes making constructive use of space, not being stuck in it. Hence the mental quirks of displaced peoples, prisoners, or travelers are in part the result of a strong self built up by assimilated diverse relationships, so that the individual has a continuing sense of location, not a dependent need of reinforcement. The city geometry delights only the untrained eye, to which the subtle patterns of the vast biome are simply invisible, the wilderness in disarray, a kind of pandemonium.[25]

Facing the decay of religious belief, says Steiner, we today tend to recreate it as best we can, including heaven and hell. But if we lack that training in looking at nature which enables us later to perceive in it the metaphors of our social concerns, and thus to value it for its poetic significance, we are left only with its literalness and with oppositions, for the final work of metaphor is to interrelate the unlike. This confusion in which the value of the nonhuman world is seen in terms of representation instead of metaphor allows us to carve our ideas into it. Instead of a guide to thought, it serves as a medium for the expression of will.

Our fear of helplessness, the perception of the cosmos and even ourselves as nonliving, and the threat of a meaningless and disordered world are all familiar complaints of the alienated modern man and, as I have suggested, are all associated with characteristic phases of psychological development. Insofar as they comprise or express our sense of a menacing disintegration, they serve a neurotic quest for control. From the self-abnegation and bodily humiliation of Christian flagellants, to the pious compulsions of fanatic cleanliness and sanitation, and finally the yearning for power over physical nature made possible by industrialized technology, we are engaged in a desperate flight from inchoate diversity and our own feelings of anonymity and fragmentation. Today we seek to fabricate a world in which we hope to heal our stunted identities and rear children in a hopeful and meaningful setting. But our rural/urban landscapes, generated by an ideology of mastery, define by subordination, not analogy. The archetypal role of nature—the mineral, plant, and animal world found most complete in wilderness—is in the development of the individual human personality, for it embodies the poetic expression of ways of being and relating to others. Urban civilization creates the illusion of a shortcut to individual maturity by attempting to omit the eight to ten years of immersion in nonhuman nature. Maturity so achieved is spurious because the individual, though he may become precociously articulate and sensitive to subtle human interplay, is without a grounding in the given structure that is nature. His grief and sense of loss seem to him to be a personality problem, so that, caught in a double bind, he will be encouraged to talk out his sense of inadequacy as though it were an interpersonal or ideological matter. Indeed, the real brittleness of modern social relationships has its roots in that vacuum where a beautiful and awesome otherness should have been encountered. The multifold otherness-with-similarities of nonhuman nature is a training ground for that delicate equilibrium between the play of likeness and difference in all social intercourse and for affirmation instead of fear of the ambiguities and liveliness of the self.

6

The Dance of
Neoteny and Ontogeny

—

Iɴ ᴛʜᴇ ɪᴅᴇᴏʟᴏɢʏ of recent times—of progress and the
self-making of the person and the society, of the ego's selection of choices of what-to-be, appended to a body—the child
is a *sac physiologique* that is fostered and that grasps or obtains
thought and intelligence. Epigenesis is a contrary concept of
life cycle (or ontogeny). The person emerges in a genetic
calendar by stages, with time-critical constraints and needs, so
that instinct and experience act in concert. The mature adult
is a late stage in this lifelong series of overlapping and inter-
locking events: not linear but spiral, resonating between disjunction and unity, but moving, so that each new cycle en-
larges the previous one.

This complicated passage through separations and symbi-
oses is human and primate. It evolved. It is based on an
extended life—extended not only by time added at the end,
but by an expanded youth. This retarded growth rate and its
associated events are neoteny. It is most conspicuous in the
slow growth of the body itself; the retention of babyish or
even fetal bone-growth patterns; toe, finger, or head orientation, reduced body-hair covering; late tooth eruption and
loss; and so on in dozens of modified organ- and tissue-

development rates. Neoteny includes a prolonged psycho-genesis. It extends, specializes, and orders experiences essential to the emergence of consciousness and the psyche.

Joseph Pearce, in his lovely book *Magical Child*, describes this emerging sense of self and separateness, the growth of a confident, centered being who reaches out to new experience, perceiving a universe in a plural reality. By symbiosis he means a connecting dependency, a kind of school for related-ness, a matrix or setting in which the structure of the world is forecast by previous experience, beginning with the body, and is discovered according to "expectations." The infant is programmed by his own nervous system to anticipate certain responses from the mother, which must be encountered in order to become the basis or matrix of the earth, a new counter-player.

Learning in this sense does not mean preparation by logi-cal operations with dialectical and ideological ends, by art appreciation or creativity, nor by overviews of history and cultures. It means a highly timed openness in which the atten-tion of the child is predirected by an intrinsic schedule, a hunger to fill archetypal forms with specific meaning. Neoteny is the biological commitment to that learning pro-gram, building identity and meaning in the oscillation be-tween autonomy and unity, separateness and relatedness. It takes about 30 percent of the whole human life span. It is a pulse, presenting the mind with wider wholes, from womb to mother and body, to earth, to cosmos. Each of these resolves tasks given in the growth of consciousness and intuition in infancy, childhood, and youth. Their goal is not to perpetuate the prenatal subjective merger state but, in a staircase of mergers and departures, to identify a self (or selves: a resolu-tion of the inchoate "we," "they," and "it" as well as "I"), leading to a more mature sense of relatedness. In this way a good sense of being in the cosmos is the result of two decades

Ontogeny and Earth Relations: *The To and Fro of Autonomy and Symbiosis*

Approximate Age	Autonomous Phase	Symbiotic Phase
20 years	mature sense of the separate self; individuation as the prologue to further epigenesis	bonds to the young and the community as leaders, parents, and elders
16th to 19th year		
13th to 15th year	regressive, transformative, idiomatic independence in dependence; ecstatic venture; solitary trial; bold isolation	eco- and socio-kinships; the metaphorical leap to cosmology
8th to 12th year		
3rd to 7th year	the ventures of cognitive autonomy; the inventory of things and their constituents	the earth matrix; terrain symbiosis based on place and natural history
2nd to 24th month		the maternal matrix; focused on the mother's face and on the body
Conception to 2nd postnatal month	pre- and postnatal autonomy; a subjective oneness	

The Epigenetic Spiral

leftward separates and identifies, to the right relates and connects of timed events that involve the person with others and with the nonhuman in an extraordinary interplay. Generally speaking, social bonds (infant-mother, juvenile-family, adolescent-community) accompany the successive matrices of being, as the ground from which novelty is explored and the self delineated, while ecological reality (flowers-bees, bears-salmon) become satisfying otherness in their own right and metaphorical sign images or messages about the inner world, the binding forces of human society, and the invisible spiritual realm.

The success of this sequence depends on good nurturing. Thus the evolution of infantile stages is accompanied by the emergence of a parental and social capacity. To be the caretakers of such a highly specialized ontogeny is itself a complex task requiring successive appropriate responses and anticipation. Neoteny as such is only the plunge into immaturity. Delivery into maturity depends on certain unique characteristics in the human adult that have been called the capacity for culture. Much of the transmitted content and behaviors making up the characteristic features of a particular people are directed to the ontogeny of its members. The details of this material—the language, myths, tools, and ceremonies—vary from one people to the next, but the differences are on the surface; they fill forms that the species has long since evolved as firmly as its physical traits.

The complexity of human development is so great and the scope for error so broad that we might wonder how anyone gets through to full maturity. Some repair processes are built into its calendar. The most conspicuous is adolescent regression, an infantile aspect that may serve the individual in recuperative ways. Beyond that, psychotherapy (which occurs in some forms in all societies) is usually shaped around a reexperiencing that enables the patient to adjust to, if not mend, a psychodevelopmental flaw. The catalysts of mind, provided by the nurturers, are like the nutritional and hormonal factors of the neotenic body, except that they are required experiences. Like the timed events in a play (either dramatic dialogue or the execution of movements in a game), they may be poorly presented, muffed, or missed.[1] The play goes on, more or less imperfectly. The person, so deprived, bears the consequences as unregenerate elements of immaturity, glossed by repression and compensation, distorted by unconscious yearnings for overdue fulfillment and resentments against the nurturers. If, for example, there was no adequate earth matrix in the child's life between its fourth and tenth year, it can never achieve a fully satisfying philosophical rapprochement to the stellar universe or to any of the fundamental questions to which religion is always directed. The cosmic counterplayers are likely to be perceived in some disguised form of infantile symbiosis, imperfectly integrated with the vast middle ground of the earth terrain and its living forms.

In the foregoing chapters I have attempted to show how each of four epochs of the past of civilized man were served by deforming the ontogeny of its members. These effects have been cumulative, but the first epoch—agriculture—was the most decisive. Unlike the society of prototypical human beings, who lived by hunting and gathering, agriculture favored larger groups of people, who, in terms of individual personality, accepted decision-making by other means than councils of the whole, the rewarded of success by power rather than prestige, and authoritarian leadership, seized rather than granted. Politically, agriculture required a society composed of members with the acumen of children. Empirically, it set about amputating and replacing certain signals and experiences central to early epigenesis. Agriculture not only infantilized animals by domestication, but exploited the infantile human traits of the normal individual neoteny.[2] The obedience demanded by the organization necessary for anything larger than the earliest village life, associated with the rise of a military caste, is essentially juvenile and submissive, reflecting proud but unreflecting loyalty, blood-brother same-sex bonding, group adventurist attitudes, tight conformism, and willingness to suffer and endure based on pride.[3] The abandonment of the totemic use of wild plants and animals and the congeniality of the ecosystem as a model for social speculating threw the mythopoetic leap to philosophy in adolescence back upon familial models, including domesticated-animal subordinates. Agriculture removed the means by which men could contemplate themselves in any other than terms of themselves (or machines). It projected back upon nature an image of human conflict and competition and then read analogies from that to people (or, as Levi-Strauss puts it, "naturalized a true culture falsely").

> The result of this is that human groups foreign to one's own are read as other species, and, on the historical misconstruction of nature as violent, the displacement, enslavement, and killing of the others is logical. One enacts rather than thinks the role of predator or prey. The poetic energies of puberty are deflected from their confrontation with the cosmic and nonhuman toward which that ontogeny had been directed for a million years, turning it back in myths that disguised the maternal symbiosis in celestial dress. In short, the unfulfilled maternal symbiosis of infant and mother leaves a vacuum that can be exploited to draw the new birth of adolescence backward, framing the world in terms of the myths of the Great Mother. While there is no doubt that the maternal symbiosis of infancy is fundamental to all further at-homeness, it is its coherence that is paradigmatic, not its enfolding, shielding, comforting surrender of responsibility. As William Thompson has pointed out, the social consequences of the prevailing myth of the Great Mother are the takeover by an even greater father.[4]

The correction of our modern abuse of the feminine and

the recovery of rootedness in the earth is not an adult adoption of the subjectivity of early development. Simply magnified, the latter carries with it all that passive, mindless lack of understanding and questing for which the ancient Mesopotamian agrotheocracies were scorned by the Hebrews and the Greeks. It is not the recovery of mother fixation, with its ambivalence of hating and adoring, fearing separation and yet resenting maternal power, that we now need, for the ideologizing of that ambiguity leads to splitting everything, a kind of final divisiveness.

A broader sensitivity to the feminine rather than fixation on mother is the normal characteristic of the child's maternal symbiosis. The intense bonding of mother and infant involves not only body contact and feeding on demand, but time together in quiet repose and leisure, during which the tentative explorations of the child away from the mother are successful to the extent that she is available and attentive, though not fussy and directing. With the beginning of village life, the number of children born to a woman in her lifetime increased from four or five to as many as sixteen (with about 50 percent survival in both). The mother could give less attention and less milk to each individual baby. Not going so far afield as her foraging counterpart, she did not carry the infant as much and was more likely to seek surrogate caretakers. The resulting failure of symbiotic bonding is unity pathology: the fearful, tentative, slow-thinking, psychologically crippled child whose personality will always be marked by a stressful mother attachment, unrelieved by a new centering in the plural earth matrix. Moreover, it does not end with the schizoid deformities of the adult, but in adults who are sick mothers, whose infants, says Harold F. Searles, "strive to remain fragmented as therapy for her and, failing, achieve inadequate separation from her and eventually from the nonhuman."[5] Failure of separation makes self and parts of the world subjectively interchangeable or, at the other extreme, dichotomized and opposing. In both there is a failure of relational factors in a literal, fragmented world without metaphorical dimension.

The fantasies, anxieties, and hostilities of unresolved immaturity are acted on or repressed and redirected in many ways. In this dark shadow of adult youthfulness is an enduring grief, a tentative feeling about the universe as though it were an incompetent parent, and a thin love of nature over deep fears. What agriculture discovered was not only that plants and animals could be subordinated, but that large numbers of men could be centrally controlled by manipulating these stresses, perpetuating their timorous search for protection, their dependence, their impulses of omnipotence and helplessness, irrational surges of adulation and hate, submission to authority, and fear of the strange.[6]

This useful warping and impedance of epigenesis in the service of village life has continued to provide mankind with a solipsistic psychology appropriate to a man-made world and its defense against neighbors. Still, its deformities are hurtful. Civilized men have pursued redress and maturity while at the same time bending ontogeny in new ways to suit new ideologies. The desert fathers, reacting against the momism of the Bronze-Age Near East, formulated patriarchy. Wrathfully demythologizing, deritualizing, and desacralizing the earth, fostering mobility and the iconography of the Word, the Hebrew prophets, Christian purists, and Hellenic Greeks sought to wrench the human personality into a more grown-up style. Taking a cue from the ontogenetic principle of the masculine guide or spirit as mediator in the transition from one symbiotic plateau to another, they misconstrued it as maleness and amputated the passage. The sense of individual responsibility fostered by these Western progenitors, resembling the juvenile's superego, and their precepts of alienation from the earth caught up the idealizing adolescent, shorn of his karma of ceremonial initiation, his dreams and emotions directed into visions of power and escape.

Repudiating myth in content and ritual act, western man broke bonds with the earth, soil, and nature, to return power to the father, and dissociated the human spirit from seasons and celestial rounds. To do so was to awaken fear of the body and world in their rhythms and inherent liveliness, to make man alien, to glorify separation anxiety. Perception and philosophy at the desert edge confirmed a split universe, sentencing the person to a lifetime of ambiguity and forcing personal identity at the terrible cost of unrelatedness. "As a prize for certified adulthood, the fathers all limit and forestall some frightening potentialities of development dangerous to 'the system'," says Erikson.[7]

In spite of their mockery of the heathen myths and ceremonies of initiation, these alienists created for their children an atmosphere of intense crises of belief and faith—matters traditionally supervised by men, even among the agricultural theocracies with their maternal symbolism. These desert patriarchs, scorning natural symbols, minimizing the plant, animal, seasonal, earthy, and feminine, exploited the adolescent capacity for abstraction—and made it terminal—by despising all such sources except the Bible and its exegesis.[8]

Both Mircea Eliade and J. L. Henderson have argued that adolescent initiation is the cultural response to an intrinsic need.[9] The desire to prove oneself, infantilisms, idealism, poeticising, and enlarged search for a new identity are age-grade traits. The tutorials, ceremonies, religious instruction, and vision inducing are administered by a cadre of adults who are themselves the product of the successful marriage of ontogeny and liturgical art. That marriage is at the heart of human cultural behavior. It is the response to the neotenic psychology of the young by mature adults. As part of the biology of human life, the ceremonies of initiation have an ecological function: they are the branch whose flowering completes a crucial phase of the life cycle by using the realm of nature as the language of religious thought. The natural world can become, in retrospect, an object of veneration if it is first an object of thought, as the prototype of coherence— and it is that because of the quality of early maternal care.

The West of the Protestant-mechanist era coupled that desert thought, with its attachment to an adolescent, ascetic, idealist escapism, to scientific mechanism and literary secular humanism in a further assault on the spirit of the autochthonous and feminine that form the basis of place attachment in every individual.

The Protestant puritanical reformulation of the self-chosen and child-inflicted alienated consciousness of the Christian fathers and Hebrew prophets had its own twists and quirks—which can also be seen as an unconscious struggle to recover maturity. One was their ambivalence about the sordidness of the organic realm. Their contempt for the body and their revulsions against the pullulations of life and the horror of slime, decay, excretion, birth, and death are not rational disinclinations, but the effects of a harshly built psychological distortion of childhood delivered up to adult consensus and rationalization. But, like the child, the Protestants were fascinated by the body in their obsessive "play" with it and its products, which ontogeny offers as proof and elements of the livingness of the self, made whole by progressive inclusionist perception.[10] Lacking that perception and affirmation of plurality and diversity it simply decays into duality.

In the pubertal youth this fixation on the body stirs with renewed force. In tribal peoples its "dirty" side is elevated to serve as a basis for pollution taboos, linking contamination to the inadequate observation of cultural practices and the adolescent drive for the purity of a shining idealism to social customs. Aversion serves a limited but positive function in group consciousness.

But if contamination is everywhere—as it is in the ideology of the puritanical version of the Fall—the metaphor becomes destructive.[11] Conditioned to despise and distrust his own intuitions regarding the body, the individual cannot incorporate a "wisdom of the body" in a philosophy of holism. The alternatives open to a society intervening in ontogeny in this way simply play out the opposition that remains unresolved by extrapolating from either the perverse, infantile, erotic pleasure of self-attention or the prudish, horrified distaste for any natural gratifications: thus Protestant culture in North America produces the world's most devoted protectors of wildlife, its greatest leaders in conservation, its most romantic wilderness literature, the first national parks, and the angriest opponents of the soiling of air and water . . . and it produces an ecological holocaust, the raping of a whole continent of forests and rich soils by uncomprehending destroyers, wrapped in patriotism, humanism, progress, and other slogans in which they profoundly believe.

The adherents to both ends of this psychoideological spectrum act out their feelings, fulfilling the modern commonplace that "man makes his environment." The psychotic, says Edith Jacobson, tries to "change the world" to meet his needs, a fantasy of performing (as opposed to symbolizing) his impulses. International corporations exult in advertising that they are changing the world. Beneath that proud boast is a kind of protean mania, advising us that we must progress or fall backward. Such fear of regression, says Jacobson, is most acute in early adolescence, when the youth, on the verge of recapitulating infantile modes of renewal, is poised psychologically between "dedifferentiation" and the movement toward maturity. The reformist environmentalist can be equally unconsciously, desperately acting out that changing of the world as the mode of changing the self, particularly in animal protectionism, wild-area (as opposed to the rest of the planet) preservation, escapist naturism, and beautification—all of which maintain two worlds, hating compromise and confusing the issues with good or evil in people.

The trouble with the eagerness to make a world is that, being already made, what is there must first be destroyed. Idealism, whether of the pastoral peaceable kingdom or the electronic paradise of technomania and outer space, is in the above sense a normal part of adolescent dreaming, like the juvenile fantasies of heroic glory. Norman Kiell observes that the "pubescent" is called on to reform while his precognitive self is at the world center, hence acts to "save mankind from his own nonhuman status"—that is, from the temporary identity vacuum in the transition from the juvenile stage into adult life.[12] The difficulty for our time is that no cultus exists, with its benign cadre of elders, to guide and administer that transition.

And so we come to our own time. And the same questions are asked: To what extent does the technological/urban society work because its members are ontogenetically stuck? What are the means and the effects of this psychological amputation? We inherit the past and its machinations. White, European-American, Western peoples are separated by many generations from decisions by councils of the whole, small-group nomadic life with few possessions, highly developed initiation ceremonies, natural history as everyman's vocation, a total surround of non–man-made (or "wild") otherness with spiritual significance, and the "natural" way of mother and infant. All these are strange to us because we are no longer competent to live them—although that competence is potentially in each of us.

The question of our own disabilities of ontogeny cannot be answered simply as the cumulative invasions into it of the past. The culture of urban technicity works out its own deformities of ontogenesis. Some of these are legacies, while others are innovative shifts in the selective perpetuation of infantile and juvenile concerns. Many aspects of the urban hive are shaped by the industries of transportation, energy use, and state-of-the art synthesis of materials and products. On the other hand, the city is shaped, designed consciously and unconsciously, by identity cripples, deprived in various social and ecological dimensions, yet also cripples in the sense of potential capacity, the possibilities of personal realization in the archaic and magnificent environments of the deep past.

Whether blindness is pathological to those living in a cave depends on whether you think of it in terms of personal adaptability or of the inherent potentialities of every member of our species. My view is the latter, but adaptability is the more vaunted trait—adaptability, that is, in the sense of flexibility, readiness to change jobs, addresses, beliefs, celebrated by the technocratic ideal of progress in convenience, comfort, safety, insulation, and the stimulus of novelty. This kind of adaptability is not of a citizenship that transcends place and time, but of not yet being adapted, of never finding one's place or time.

Cultural anthropology has often been used as evidence of this contemporary notion of heroic flexibility. A great many ethnographic studies do impress us with the various ways of being human, but few of them emphasize the inexorable direction in all human societies: what all cultures seek is to clarify and confirm the belongingness of their members, even at the expense of perpetuating infantile fears, of depriving the members of the object of their quest for adaptedness and making their only common ground their nonrootedness.

In this connection it is no surprise that the "adaptability

society" celebrates childhood, admires youth and despises age, and equates childhood with innocence, wisdom, and spiritual power. Its members cling to childhood, for their own did not serve its purpose. To those for whom adult life is admixed with decrepit childhood, the unfulfilled promise cannot be abandoned. To wish to remain childlike, to foster the nostalgia for childhood, is to grieve for our own lost maturity, not because maturity is synonymous with childhood, but because then it was still possible to move, epigenetically, toward maturity.

Wide-eyed wonder, nonjudgmental response, and the immediate joy of being are beautiful to see; I hope some kernel of them remains in the heart of every adult. They are sometimes presented as appropriate models for adult attitudes toward nature. But the open ecstasy of the child has its special purposes: a kind of cataloging, preconscious order-finding, and cryptic anthropomorphizing that have to do with personality development—at least for the child with a good mother bond. The poorly bonded child goes through this nature-wonder period even though troubled, for it is a new "maternal" reality and perhaps is therapeutic. In any case, there is no figurative nature for the child; all is literal. Even in pretending, there is only one reality. The children playing delightedly on the green grass or in awe at an owl in the woods will grow up oblivious to the good in nature if they never go beyond that momentary fascination. When, as adults, they will weigh the literal value of the owl (already realized, for it taught them the name and owlness) against other literal values, such as replacing the forest with a hospital, a sewage system, or an oil well, their judgment is likely to be for progress. With poor initial mother symbiosis, with an inadequate or lackluster place and creature naturizing, or without the crucial adolescent religious initiation that uses the symbiotic, literal world as a prefigured cosmos, the adult cannot choose the forest and the owl. His self is still at the center of a juvenile reality. It may be true that the purpose of the childlike pleasure in the outdoors is an end in itself; it is also necessary to the further work of the self going beyond the self.

But I have oversimplified the choices in order to make a point. There is not a choice between the owl and the oil well at all. In our society those who would choose the owl are not more mature. Growing out of Erikson's concept of trust versus nontrust as an early epigenetic concern and out of the Russells' observation that the child perceives poor nurturing as hostility—which is either denied and repressed (as among idealists) or transferred in its source so as to be seen as coming from the natural world instead of from the parents (as among cynics)—there arises an opposition that is itself an extension of infantile duality. Fear and hatred of the organic on one hand, the desire to merge with it on the other; the impulse to control and subordinate on one hand, to worship the nonhuman on the other; overdifferentiation on one hand, fears of separation on the other: all are two sides of a coin. In the shape given to a civilization by totemically inspired, technologically sophisticated, small-group, epigenetically fulfilled adults, the necessity to choose would never arise.

In effect, the four historical episodes in such socially assimilated deprivation have become elements in the European-American personality. The American is not the profligate anti-European; he is, in respect to certain characteristics, the full embodiment of Western, classical, Christian man, enabled by the colossal richness of an unexploited continent to play out the savaging of neoteny according to the agendas of domestication, desert-edge transcendence, Galilean-Calvinist dualities, and industrialization. Careless of waste, wallowing in refuse, exterminating the enemies, having everything now and new, despising age, denying human natural history, fabricating pseudotraditions, swamped in the repeated personal crises of the aging preadolescent: all are familiar images of American society. They are the signs of private nightmares of incoherence and disorder in broken climaxes where technologies in pursuit of mastery create ever-worsening problems—private nightmares expanded to a social level.

All Westerners are heir, not only to the self-justifications of recent technophilic Promethean impulses, but to the legacy of the whole. Men may now be the possessors of the world's flimsiest identity structure, the products of a prolonged tinkering with ontogenesis—by Paleolithic standards, childish adults. Because of this arrested development, modern society continues to work, for it requires dependence. But the private cost is massive therapy, escapism, intoxicants, narcotics, fits of destruction and rage, enormous grief, subordination to hierarchies that exhibit this callow ineptitude at every level, and, perhaps worst of all, a readiness to strike back at a natural world that we dimly perceive as having failed us. From this erosion of human nurturing comes the failure of the passages of the life cycle and the exhaustion of our ecological accords.

In the city world of today, infinite wants are pursued as though the environment were an amnion and technology a placenta. Unlike the submissive cultures of obedience, those of willful, proud disengagement, or those obsessed with guilt and pollution, this made world is the home of omnipotence and immediate satisfaction. There is no mother of limited resources or disciplining father, only a self in a fluid system.

The high percentage of neuroses in Western society seems often to be interpreted as a sign of a highly stressful "lifestyle." If you add to it—or see it acted out as—the insanities of nationalism, war, and biome busting, a better case than simply that of lifestyle can be made in terms of an epidemic of the psychopathic mutilation of ontogeny. Characteristic of the schizoid features of this immature subjectivity is difficulty differentiating among fantasy, dream, and reality. The inability to know whether one's experiences originate in night dreaming, daydreaming, or viridical reality is one of the most familiar disabilities of seriously ill mental patients. Drug use and New Age psychedelic athletics in search of a different reality, even the semantics of using "fantasy" as synonymous with creative imagination and "to dream" as inspiration, suggest an underlying confusion. They are like travesties of the valid adolescent karma, the religious necessity of transcendence. The fears associated with this confusion in adults are genuinely frightening. The anguished yearning for something lost is inescapable for those not in psychiatric care or on weekend psychic sprees, but who live daily in time-serving labor, overdense groups, and polluted surroundings. Blurry aspirations are formulated in concealed infantilisms, mediated in spectator entertainment, addiction to worldwide news, and religious revivalism.

Much of this has been said before, but not so often in terms of the relationship of the human to the nonhuman. Even as socially intense as we are, much of the unconscious life of the individual is rooted in interaction with otherness that goes beyond our own kind, interacting with it very early in personal growth, not as an alternative to human socialization, but as an adjunct to it. The fetus is suspended in water, tuned to the mother's chemistry and the biological rhythms that are keyed to the day and seasonal cycles. The respirational interface between the newborn and the air imprints a connection between consciousness (or wisdom) and breath. Gravity sets the tone of all muscle and becomes a major counterplayer in all movement. Identity formation grows from the subjective separation of self from not-self, living from nonliving, human from nonhuman, and proceeds in speech to employ plant and animal taxonomy as a means of conceptual thought and as a model of relatedness. Games and stories involving animals serve as projections for the discovery of the plurality of the self. The environment of play, the juvenile home range, is the gestalt and creative focus of the face or matrix of nature. Ordeals in wilderness solitude and the ecological patterns underlying the protophilosophical narration of myth are instruments in the maturing of the whole person.

Only in the success of this extraordinary calendar does the adult come to love the world as the ground of his being. As a child, immersed in the series of maternal/ecological matrices, there are inevitable normal anxieties, distorted perceptions, gaps in experience filled with fantasy, emotional storms full of topical matter, frightening dreams and illusions, groundless fears, and the scars of accident, occasional nurturing error, adult negligence, and cruelty. The risk of epigenesis is that the nurturers and caretakers do not move forward in their role in keeping with the child's emerging stages. If such deprivations are severe enough, the normal fears and fantasies can become enduring elements of the personality. The individual continues to act on some crucial moment in the immense concerns of immaturity: separation, otherness, and limitation. Wrestling with them in juvenile and primary modes, even the adult cannot possibly see them holistically. Some of these omissions and impairments enhance the individual's conformity to certain cultures, and the culture acts to reward them, to produce them by interceding in the nurturing process, and so put a hold on development. In this way, juvenile fantasies and primary thought are articulated not only in the monosyllables of the land scalper, but in philosophical argument and pontifical doctrine. Irrational feelings may be escalated into high-sounding reason when thrown up against a seemingly hostile and unfulfilling natural world. The West is a vast testimony to childhood botched to serve its own purposes, where history, masquerading as myth, authorizes men of action and men of thought to alter the world to match their regressive moods of omnipotence and insecurity.

The modern West selectively perpetuates these psychopathic elements. In the captivity and enslavement of plants and animals and the humanization of the landscape itself is the diminishment of the Other, against which men must define themselves, a diminishment of schizoid confusion in self-identity. From the epoch of Judeo-Christian emergence is an abiding hostility to the natural world, characteristically fearful and paranoid. The sixteenth-century fixation on the impurity of the body and the comparative tidiness of the machine are strongly obsessive-compulsive. These all persist and interact in a tapestry of chronic madness in the industrial present, countered by dreams of absolute control and infinite possession.

There are two ways of seeing this overall sequence. One is a serial amputation of the maturing process, in which the domesticated world and dichotomous desert deflected adolescent initiation and rigidified the personality in clinging to the collective loyalties, feats of bravery, and verbal idealism of pubertal youth. The era of puritans and machines fixated on childhood anxiety about the body and its productions. The urban/industrial age keyed on infantile identity diffusions, separation fears, and the fantasies of magic power. These truncations of epigenesis are progressive amputations, first at adolescence and finally at infancy.

Alternatively, the initial domestication may be seen as a calamity for human ontogeny against which subsequent history is marked by cultural efforts to recover a mature perspective without giving up the centralization of power made possible by unleashing fecundity and urban huddling. In this sense, history is characterized as the will to recover the grace and poise of the mature individual, initially reduced to a shambles by the neolithic, without giving up the booty. For example, the psychology of self-actualization, group dynamics, and personal therapy, aimed at healing individuals deprived of appropriate adolescent religious experience, though helpful to the individual, is basically antagonistic to the modern state, which needs fearful followers and slogan-shouting idealists. Thus the culture counters these identity therapies and the philosophical realism of a cosmopolitan and sophisticated kind that could result from them with prior wounds—damage to the fetus and neonate in hospital birth, through the anxieties of the distraught mother, asphyxiation, anesthetics, premedication, the overwhelming sensory shock of bright lights, noisy surroundings, and rough handling, impairment of delivery by the mother's physical condition and delivery posture, and separation of the infant from the mother—all corroding the psychogenic roots of a satisfactory life in a meaningful world.[13]

What can one say of the prospect of the future in a world where increasing injury to the planet is a symptom of human psychopathology? Is not the situation far worse than one of rational choices in an economic system or the equilibration of competing vested interests?

In some ways the situation is far more hopeful. An ecologically harmonious sense of self and world is not the outcome of rational choices. It is the inherent possession of everyone; it is latent in the organism, in the interaction of the genome and early experience. The phases of such early experiences, or epigenesis, are the legacy of an evolutionary past in which human and nonhuman achieved a healthy rapport. Recent societies have contorted that sequence, have elicited and perpetuated immature and inappropriate responses. The societies are themselves the product of such amputations, and so are their uses and abuses of the earth.

Perhaps we do not need new religious, economic, technological, ideological, esthetic, or philosophical revolutions. We may not need to start at the top and uproot political systems, turn life-ways on their heads, emulate hunters and gatherers or naturalists, or try to live lives of austere privation or tribal organization. The civilized ways inconsistent with human maturity will themselves wither in a world where children move normally through their ontogeny.

I have attempted to identify crucial factors in such a normal growth by showing what might have been lost from different periods in the past. Some of these, such as life in a small human group in a spacious world, will be difficult to recover —though not impossible for the critical period in the individual passage. Adults, weaned to the wrong music, cut short from their own potential, are not the best of mentors. The problem may be more difficult to understand than to solve. Beneath the veneer of civilization, to paraphrase the trite phrase of humanism, lies not the barbarian and animal, but the human in us who knows the rightness of birth in gentle surroundings, the necessity of a rich nonhuman environment, play at being animals, the discipline of natural history, juvenile tasks with simple tools, the expressive arts of receiving food as a spiritual gift rather than as a product, the cultivation of metaphorical significance of natural phenomena of all kinds, clan membership and small-group life, and the profound claims and liberation of ritual initiation and subsequent stages of adult mentorship. There is a secret person undamaged in every individual, aware of the validity of these, sensitive to their right moments in our lives. All of them are assimilated in perverted forms in modern society: our profound love of animals twisted into pets, zoos, decorations, and entertainment; our search for poetic wholeness subverted by the model of the machine instead of the body; the moment of pubertal idealism shunted into nationalism or ethereal otherworldly religion instead of an ecosophical cosmology.

But this means that we have not lost, and cannot lose, the genuine impulse. It awaits only an authentic expression. The task is not to start by recapturing the theme of a reconciliation with the earth in all of its metaphysical subtlety, but with something much more direct and simple that will yield its own healing metaphysics.

Notes

Preface

1. *The Mask of Sanity* (St. Louis: C. V. Mosby, 1976).
2. "Psychological Development and Historical Change," in Robert Jay Lifton, ed., *Explorations in Psychohistory* (New York: Simon & Schuster, 1974).

1. Introduction

1. Quoted by Thaddis W. Box, "Range Deterioration in West Texas," *Southwestern Historical Quarterly* 71, no. 1 (July 1967).
2. Of these normal human environments, John Calhoun says, "Evolutionary history modified physiology to demand a given rate of contact in harmony with having lived in a particular group size in a particular habitat. Man is no exception. Through most of his evolution he has lived in relatively closed groups of relatively small size. There are reasons to believe that man lies along an evolutionary path on which the optimum group size (of adult members) has a range of seven to nineteen with a mean of twelve" ("Ecological Factors in the Development of Behavioral Anomalies," in Joseph Zubin and Howard F. Hunt, eds., *Comparative Psychopathology: Animal and Human* [New York: Grune & Stratton, 1967]).

2. The Domesticators

1. The best evidence for the ponderous emergence of agriculture is the carbon-14 dating of the oldest-known samples of the

various domesticated plants and animals. Most of the community of cultivated forms does not appear in the first seven thousand years (Colin Renfrew, *Before Civilization: The Radiocarbon Revolution and Prehistoric Europe* [London: Cambridge University Press, 1979]).

Adina Kabaker, "A Radiocarbon Chronology Relevant to the Origins of Agriculture," 957–980 in Charles A Reed, ed., *Origins of Agriculture* (The Hague: Mouton Publishers, 1977).

2. José Ortega y Gasset, *Meditations on Hunting* (New York: Scribner's, 1972), p. 150. The idea of "attention" overlaps both anecdotal and technical approaches. It can be seen as a cultural style, as in Ortega y Gasset, or as an organizing concept in neuropsychological processes. If the hunter's attention was in some sense "superior" then perhaps the question is whether it touches on child rearing for us today. For the scientific end of this spectrum, see Monte Jay Meldman, *Diseases of Attention and Perception* (New York: Pergamon Press, 1970).

3. Phenology, like taxonomy, in contrast to the more trendy forms of nature study in behavior or ecology, does not have a lively press. But it is what the mature naturalist finally comes to. Much of Henry Thoreau's journal in the nineteenth century, like the work of Aldo Leopold in the twentieth, is given to the dates of first appearance—of flowers blooming, the passage of migratory birds, and so on. It is not that these topics are actually less dynamic than the more dramatic aspects of nature, but that their liveliness depends on a deeper understanding and a more refined sense of mystery.

4. Place to Australian aborigines is not a detachable quality or an abstract way of making location a relative commodity. It is continuous with the identity structure of the adult. It is embedded there as a result of a combination of daily life and formal ceremony during the first fifteen to twenty years of life. It is not unreasonable to suppose that something like it gave shape to the religious life and the personality of the prehistoric hunter-gatherers of Eurasia and Africa. A major study of the role of place in the mental and emotional growth of the individual among present-day hunters or among American Indian tribes has not, to my knowledge, been done. For the Australians, see Amos Rapoport, "Australian Aborigines and the Definition of

Place," in William Mitchell, ed., *Environmental Design: Research and Practice* (Los Angeles: University of California Press, 1972).

5. Defensive personal space is analogous to territoriality in animal breeding space. The most scholarly work on the latter remains Robert Ardrey's *The Territorial Imperative: A Personal Inquiry into the Animal Origins of Property and Nations* (New York: Atheneum, 1966). However, since that book, studies of the territoriality of tribal peoples tend to show something rather different from exclusive occupancy of space or warlike stance concerning boundaries, something directed more toward particular resources and symbolic means of avoiding conflict. Ardrey's leap from typical animal territoriality to human war as equally normal was unjustified: organized human invasion by force is probably due to the breakdown of human social behavior rather than its healthy expression. Since the "natural" processes associated with social disintegration are psychological, it seems likely that they are also regressive and infantile.

6. The making of boundaries in a deforested terrain is done in terms of familiar landforms or, lacking those, man-made rock piles. Jane Ellen Harrison long ago pointed out that the "worship of stones" originated as "boundary" markers between the living and the dead. "Hermes is at first just a Herm, a stone or pillar set up to commemorate the dead. . . . In his lifetime a man went to his father or his grandfathers, to his elders for advice. . . . If the worshipper is an agriculturist his desire will be for his seeds and the Herm will be the guardian of his crops. But if he be a shepherd not less will he look to his dead ancestor to be the guardian of his sheep, to make them be fruitful and multiply. So when the Herm gets a head and gradually becomes wholly humanized, among a pastoral people he carries on his shoulders a ram, and from the Ram Carrier, the Criophorus, Christianity has taken her Good Shepherd" (Jane Ellen Harrison, *Mythology* [New York: Cooper Square, 1963], pp. 11–12; see also Nelson Gulic, *Rivers in the Desert: A History of the Negev* [New York: Farrar, 1959], p. 229).

7. The Great Mother Earth has been described at length in many works, notably those by Eric von Neumann, Joseph Campbell, Homer Smith, Henri Frankfort, Mircea Eliade, and Simone de

Beauvoir. No single figure is more indicative of the tendency of farming peoples to extrapolate their place in the cosmos from the symbiosis between infant and mother. The nature of ritual reenactment and its use of regressive psychological states ensures that the force of such an image draws directly from the powerful unconscious memories of individual infancy. Whether or not the dependencies, emotional states, and metaphors inspired by early experience suffuse a society in immaturity and incompetence may depend on what the "benign elders" do with that inspiration in the initiation of adolescents and the education of young adults. If the goddess is seen as erratically undependable and possessive, she may hold her "children" in infantile bondage. If she is perceived as the model of a matrix that her children carry away with them as an understanding of the world, then she may have served to liberate them to further growth.

Harrison tells us that, like Hermes, "all the other gods ... had the like lowly parentage" of being first only stones and "later surmounted by a head" (*Mythology*, p. 6). One may wonder whether the increasing anthropomorphism of the goddess over the centuries of early agriculture did not make it more difficult for the child to project the maternal spirit onto nature in general. Or, put another way, if the Earth Mother were represented in the actual figure of a woman, would this not interfere with the child's ability to transfer to the earth the metaphor of mother and to get stuck instead with a re-presentment of her? My tentative answer here is yes, and therefore what is regarded historically as the evolution of the gods by increased anthropomorphism was what psychologists call "dedifferentiation," a poorer discrimination and dependency on someone else's powers of authoritative discernment.

8. Representation of the gods as humanlike among Hindus, Mayans, ancient Greeks, and many other cultures often shows them riding on certain animals. While the meaning of the mounted god is beyond our scope, it may be said that no mounted figures appear before domestication and that they occur in hierarchic, anthropomorphizing religions. Spiritual diversity is represented increasingly by social, rather than special or ecological, diversity. The transition is represented by

the riding-on, which connects the personhood of the god with his appropriate ancestral animalhood. The effect is a closure of metaphysical imagery, a retreat from the world-at-large as signifying or symbolizing. To ride on is, after all, to be once again carried. The similarity of this to a more childish perceptual style is unavoidable.

9. R. E. Money-Kryle and others believe paradise to be the sub-adult's re-vision of the "disappearing breast." The whole literature of paradise is fraught with mammary allusions (R. E. Money-Kryle, *Man's Picture of His World* [London: Duckworth, 1968], p. 50). Harold F. Searles discusses Hudson's *Green Mansions* as an adolescent fantasy. The ideal of purity, he says, is akin to childish love of one's mother. From it, in late childhood, arises idealized nature as part of a similar projection. Maturity is a relinquishment of this view. "In *Green Mansions* Abel, I believe, fails to carry through to this final differentiation of himself as a full-fledged human being. Those persons who, like Abel, fail to make this final achievement of normal adolescence apparently continue throughout their lives to identify themselves more with Nature than with mankind" (*The Nonhuman Environment in Normal Development and in Schizophrenia* [New York: International Universities Press, 1960], p. 99). One is tempted to point the finger at naturalists, nature lovers, preservationists, and so on—but perhaps prematurely. Elsewhere Searles (p. 395) and others point out that inadequate mothering may result in the individual's lifelong overdependence on objects in the search for his own mature identity. If this means materialism, accumulating and hoarding of things, and identity by acquisition, then the technocratic wasters of nature today have no reason to snort down their noses at the romantic childishness of those who sometimes seem to confuse wilderness with paradise.

10. The idea of a declining world is reviewed in Clarence Glacken's *Traces on the Rhodian Shore* (Berkeley: University of California Press, 1967, p. 379.) and is explained in Christian theology by the Fall. The Christians had abundant evidence to go on, as the Mediterranean world was physically deteriorating. According to R. O. Whyte, the destruction of the great juniper forests of Persia began after 5,000 B.C. Grazing, dry farming, and char-

coal burning turned Syria into a vast overgrazed steppe. Erosion produced the "colossal silt load of the Tigris and Euphrates," and vegetational collapse *resulted* in locust infestations. Kilns, smelters, and urban construction put further demands on the forests. Whyte adds, "For these reasons combined with the clearance of land for cultivation, the forest resources of our region were dissipated unwisely, and on a vast scale. The bald mountains and foothills of the Mediterranean littoral, the Anatolian Plateau and Iran stand as stark witnesses of millennia of uncontrolled utilization." What made it worse was increased rainfall from 5,000 to 2,000 B.C., which cushioned the effects of land abuse somewhat, followed by two thousand years of profound aridity, which aggravated them ("Evolution of Land Use in South-Western Asia," in L. Dudley Stamp, *A History of Land Use in Arid Regions,* Paris: UNESCO Arid Zone Research, vd. 17., 1961). That this deterioration was perceived as a form of pollution is not surprising. What is less accountable is that, with the spread of Western ideologies and Christianity north into Europe on the heels of agriculture, the image of a "declining" world was so convincing in spite of the rich virginal fruitfulness of the fertile lands. It is in part a testimony to the further spiritualizing and abstracting that the Christians added to the Jewish heritage that the Europeans would continue to believe until the seventeenth century that the world was worse than it had been.

11. The garden image of paradise is apparently a debased figure, in which the cultures of husbandry described a lost world, using the best landscape images they knew. But "Adam" means "red" and has to do with men of the red upland soils rather than the black cultivated ones. Geographically, Eden was a steppe plateau, the home of hunters and gatherers. The yearning that the myth first expressed must have been that of disillusioned tillers of the soil for a long-lost life of freedom and relative ease. Eventually the urban ideology of civilization, in which men defined themselves by contrast to wild savages, made the nomadic image untenable (Nigel Calder, *Eden Was No Garden: An Enquiry into the Environment of Man* [New York: Holt, Rinehart & Winston, 1967]).

12. Arnold Modell, *Object Love and Reality* (New York: International Universities Press, 1968), p. 24.

13. The distinction between grain- and root-farming cultures has been cited as the basis of fundamental differences of outlook between Occident and Orient. Briefly, the thesis is that the root crops of southeast Asia required fewer and simpler techniques of cultivation, were perennials instead of annuals, stored less well than grain, concentrated less energy than grain, were grown in small, mixed assemblages instead of large monocultures, required less irrigation, and fermented differently. The result is that the husbandry of Asia was more in harmony with the inward and passive mysteries of the feminine principle. The Great Mother in the West was more readily subordinated to the calculating and regimenting masculine ideal. Even today, the maternal figure in Asia keeps an energy that in the West was swept away by the conquest of the Mycenaeans by the Achaeans and in the Levant by the collapse of the autochthonous temple cities of the river valleys (Edwin M. Loeb, "Wine, Women and Song: Root Planting and Head Hunting," in Stanley Diamond, ed., *Culture in History* [New York: Columbia University Press, 1960]).

14. Temperate and arid tropical regions impel divergent views of fecundity itself. In the north the same generative forces making luxuriant crops and cattle can spill over as swarms of pests and malignant forms of decay. Without constant vigilance, root and vine eat away at human works, forest invades the field, and marsh and fen overwhelm man-made drains. But in the subarid subtropics, where agriculture began, fertility is more clearly benign, a counterforce to the dry and sterile nonlife. Ten millennia ago the lands east of the Mediterranean were wetter and richer than they are today, so that the environmental cues of dichotomy were muted, but they were there.

   The deep human need for name learning and classifying that emerges in the individual with speech itself continues throughout life in satisfactions rooted in our sense of order. Conversely, when categories are not so clear it is perceptually and psychologically troubling to us. I have sometimes felt that this esthetic pleasure of things-in-their-place was a strong element of the beauty of the desert fringes, where agriculture began. There each plant and each mountain is a separate being, totally visible and clearly what it is. All differences seem emphasized—day and night (with their short twilight), wet places and dry places, life and nonlife, sky and earth. The human impact on dry lands tends to further exaggerate some of these differences. While one cannot conclude from this that desert people have any less subtlety of thought, there is available to them a world of visible contrasts that may be seen as evidence of a fundamental and pervasive rule of dichotomy in the universe.

15. "An Ecological Perspective on the Eastern Pueblos," in Alfonso Ortiz, ed., *New Perspectives on the Pueblos* (Albuquerque: University of New Mexico Press, 1972); see Mircea Eliade, "Nostalgia for Paradise in Primitive Traditions," *Myths, Dreams and Mysteries* (New York: Harper & Bros., 1960), and *The Quest* (Chicago: University of Chicago Press, 1969), p. 80. Such celebrations are widely reported in which group release also found expression in sadistic spectacles: bulls and bears or death fights of men and animals. Because of the disorder in their lives, says Paul Ford, the agricultural pueblo people of Southwestern America have periodic festivals in which all rules are broken and norms of behavior violated. In these orgies the tribe dissipates its burden of dissonance and incongruity, gaining control over it by enacting it, and starts fresh from that chaos which is felt to be a necessary prelude to the rejuvenation of society, just as it is in the generation of the individual.

16. Harold F. Searles, "Non-differentiation of Ego Functioning in the Borderline Individual and Its Effect upon His Sense of Personal Identity." Paper presented at the Sixth International Symposium on the Psychotherapy of Schizophrenia, Lausanne, Switzerland, 28 September 1978.

Farmers, assuming nature to be conscious but not very bright, acted out what they wanted her to do, ritually copulating in the fields so that they, like the crops in which they saw themselves mirrored, also might be fruitful. The customary barriers to birth began to erode as larger human numbers became advantageous. The spacing of children shrank from three or four years to one, aided by a reservoir of village wet nurses (human and animal), the sedentary household, and the availability of more sitters and caretakers. The farmer and his wife engaged in an annual begetting paralleling that of the earth, a fructification supportive and symbolic of a universal process. Sixteen children in a lifetime would not be unusual (though half or fewer would live to adolescence), perhaps four times the number born to the woman in a hunting-gathering society (Richard B. Lee, "Population Growth and the Beginnings of Sedentary Life among the !Kung Bushmen," in Brian Spooner, ed., *Population Growth: Anthropological Implications* [Cambridge: Massachusetts Institute of Technology Press, 1972]).

What seems at first a convenient arrangement—mother substitutes and surrogates—can disturb the infant, sometimes with lifelong effects. The infant is normally imprinted by its own mother during the first weeks of postnatal life. Loss of the mother, even for periods of hours or days, can result, says Anthony Storr, in a permanent attachment to her, tainted by fear, distrust, reclusiveness, and the tendency to extend this tormenting connection to an ambiguous entity, such as society or the earth. Even separation for feeding may wound it with a deep and lasting grief, a distrust of the world, and a failure of courage. The gestalt—"support system"—becomes unworthy of faith, and, in anxiety lest it disappear again and again, the child fails to develop the confidence necessary for achieving the mature independence necessary to move toward a freedom from maternal symbiosis (*The Dynamics of Creation* [New York: Atheneum, 1972], pp. 69–73). To be deprived of that possibility is to remain at a vague, juvenile identity level. Thus farmers and villagers do have a strong sense of belonging to the land and become fierce patriots and willing subordinates in societies that control the food supply by controlling maternal processes, invidiously and ritually.

17. Marshall Sahlins, *Stone Age Economics* (Chicago: Aldine, 1972), pp. 11–13.
18. Searles, "Non-differentiation of Ego-Functioning."
19. John Yudkin, "Archaeology and the Nutritionist," in Peter J. Ucko and G. W. Dimbleby, eds., *The Domestication and Exploitation of Plants and Animals* (Chicago: Aldine, 1969). Richard B. Lee, "What Hunters Do for a Living, or, How to Make Out on Scarce Resources," in Richard B. Lee and Irven DeVore, eds., *Man the Hunter* (Chicago: Aldine, 1968).

It might be objected that trade and markets increased the culinary opportunities beyond the possibilities in a wilderness.

Perhaps this was true for the wealthy, but for the majority it was not. Even now, the modern supermarket, with all its opulence, has an illusory diversity. The actual kinds of fresh fruits and vegetables are extremely limited and stereotyped in plant variety. Much the same is true of meats. Even though it may be less true of canned goods, my own guess is that family buying habits are highly predictable and repetitive. Why is this so in a comparatively rich society unless it is a continuation of normal immature tastes and unconscious dependence on the literal use of food as part of a self-identity structure?

20. "The Spirit of the Gift" in Sahlins, *Stone Age Economics.*

21. A good example might be music. In conventional history/progress thinking, the complexity and quality of music have steadily grown in the course of cultural evolution from something repetitive and simple like the Kalahari bushman's plucking his bowstring to the symphonies of the nineteenth century. But a very different view is possible. Susanne Langer observes that "the great office of music is to . . . give us an insight into . . . the subjective unity of experience" by using the principle of physical biology: rhythm. Its physiological effect is to reduce inner tensions by first making them symbolically manifest, then resolving and unifying them (*Feeling and Form* [London: Routledge, 1953], p. 126). One interpretation is that the more complex the music, the more fundamental the problem; or, one might say, the more elaborate the music, the more fragmented the vision of the world. Composer and musician Paul Winter has said that we are now habituated to an overstructured format, especially in so-called classical music, from which we need to escape into a more informal extemporaneous performance and audition. But if, indeed, music is a kind of final refuge serving to hold things together, this might be impossible in modern life.

22. For the effects of domestication on the physique and behavior of animals, see H. Spurway, "The Causes of Domestication: An Attempt to Integrate Some Ideas of Konrad Lorenz with Evolution Theory," *Journal of Genetics* 53 (1955): 325; Erich Isaac, "On the Domestication of Cattle," *Science* 137 (1962): 195; and E. B. Hale, "Domestication and the Evolution of Behaviour" and other papers in E. S. E. Hafez, ed., *Behaviour*

of Domestic Animals (New York: Williams & Williams, 1962).

23. Wilhelm Stekel, "The Animal in Fantasy," *Patterns of Psychosexual Infantilism* (New York: Evergreen, 1959), chap. 6.

24. "The Strategy of Ecosystem Development," *Science* 164 (1969): 262–270. I am aware that the concept of the climax has fallen into disfavor among some ecologists in recent years, but it remains useful in speaking of the appearance of the world to an observer in the course of an ordinary lifetime.

25. Ortega y Gasset, *Meditations on Hunting*, p. 140–143.

26. The attendant executive diseases center around the dysfunc tional effects of protracted stress. What Searles says of the child who is given "responsibility" for events he cannot actually control is surely indicative of physiological and psychological pathology in a culture determined to "control the environment." Searles, "Non-Differentiation of Ego-Functioning in the Borderline Individual," p. 10.

27. "State of Surrender," *The Sciences* 11, no. 1 (1971). With agriculture, there arose scheduled work routines. Edith Jacobson makes the interesting observation that repetitive work conceals psychosis, which erupts when the individual leaves the job or even takes a vacation. What from one perspective seems like a form of efficient human labor may be seen from another as a kind of therapy for psychological upheavals in other aspects of life (*Psychotic Conflict and Reality* [New York: International Universities Press, 1967], p. 38).

28. This is because others in the family may use the child to complement their own defective egos (Harold F. Searles, *Countertransference* [New York: International Universities Press, 1979], pp. 175–77).

3. The Desert Fathers

1. Of course, individual historians have struggled against the rules, opposed not only by the amirs of their own field but by the whole humanistic establishment. For example, Ellsworth Huntington's theory early in the twentieth century that national traits could be in part explained by local climate appealed to a widely shared intuitive feeling for connectedness

between the human and natural. He was roughly handled by his critics, not only because some of his speculations were extreme, but because his timing was bad. He wrote as the foundations for existentialism were being laid, as reductionism dominated biology, and as the psychology of James Watson emphasized the conditioning of the individual, turning psychology toward experimental atomism and clinical manipulations. The Adlerian therapies of "making yourself," the declarations of independence from biology by the social sciences, and the repudiation of evolution as pertinent to the individual all hark back to the tabula rasa of John Locke. The theology of Karl Barth, the "new criticism" in art, and all rejection of "determinism" by intellectuals and academics built contempt for the natural history of man apart from comparative anatomy, which remained mainly useful for the training of medical students. As an undergraduate interested in what I considered the ecological aspects of human history, I was puzzled by the discontinuity between what historians and archaeologists and biological evolutionists did. Logically, I thought, the human past, an unbroken story, should be a scholarly continuum as well. The division of these disciplines in the university seemed inadequately explained as a teaching convenience. I mistakenly supposed that all that was needed were students who were willing to study more than one field, who would then become links between them. Gradually, I learned—well after I had begun to teach—that there was something internal in these fields that was hostile to the idea, and that this opposition was more than a concern for clear definitions between the particular disciplines.

2. In the light of much diligent opprobrium—and its more general expressions in popular arts, school curricula, and the entertainment and news media—the scorn for the work of Konrad Lorenz, Robert Ardrey, Desmond Morris, and Edward Wilson for their naturalization of man is not surprising. Yet the revulsion they evoke goes far deeper than contemporary culture, for they seem to strike not only at current relativism, but at more-fundamental assumptions deriving from the assertions of the desert fathers of the West: the absolute distinctions between man, nature, and the supernatural (Aldous

Huxley, "The Desert," *Tomorrow and Tomorrow and Tomorrow*, [New York: Signet, 1964]).

3. Part of the difference between the Egyptian stasis and what would become history in the minds of the Semitic sons of old Sumer is due to the differences in their rivers: the Nile flooding peacefully and cyclically, the Euphrates violently and erratically (Henri Frankfort, "Egypt: The Nature of the Universe," *The Intellectual Adventure of Ancient Man* [Chicago: University of Chicago Press, 1946]).

4. The Four Horsemen are formulated as the chief forces of history (Jacques Ellul, *Apocalypse: The Book of Revelation* [New York: Seabury, 1977]).

5. This cycle combining ecological and social bases in the rise and fall of the desert empires can be seen in the joint reading of four essays: R. O. Whyte, *op. cit.* p. 93–98; W. C. Lowdermilk, "Conquest of the Land through Seven Thousand Years," USDA Agricultural Information Bulletin No. 99 (Washington, D.C.: Soil Conservation Service, 1953); Robert L. Carneiro, "A Theory of the Origin of the State," *Science* 169 (1970): 733; and Franklin Russell, "The Road to Ur," *Horizon* 14 (1972): 90.

6. When they settled, the Hebrews were on dry marginal land instead of rich bottomlands. Even here uncertainty persisted, so that the eruptive quality of events was not reduced as it might have been by the relative certainty of crop success known to those on lower lands. This could have only perpetuated the association of morality and climate and the synonymy of failure and punishment.

7. The "desert ways" of the Kenites, Kenizzites, Calebites, Yerahmilites, and Rachabites in the Negev, says Nelson Gulic, were "idealized in the religious philosophy of Israel." These were simplicity, austerity, selflessness, "prophetic ideals"; the "leanness, clarity and uncompromising qualities of Sinai and the Southland were favorably contrasted with the abominable fertility practices and idolatry of the Canaanite civilization." Of the Negev, "the very ground became and remained the touchstone enabling the peoples of the Exodus and their descendents to find and ever renew their spiritual values." Gulic speaks of "the kind of clarity and puritanism that are characteristic of the desert atmosphere . . . the rockbound realities

of inner attitudes and concrete actions of love and mercy and justice." As a good believer and historian he concludes, "The ruins of cities and villages that litter the face of the earth as a result of mankind's savagery are more than counterbalanced by the pilgrim's progress, however painful and slow, through the march of history" (*Rivers in the Desert: A History of the Negev* [New York: Farrar, 1959], pp. 66, 141, 144).

8. "The Desert," *Collected Essays* (New York: Bantam, 1964).

9. In an unpublished and untitled, perspicacious essay written while he was a student at Williams College in 1968, David Klemm, now a professor of theology, perceived that the "environmental crisis" was, in fact, related to the concept of history. Analyzing Paul Tillich's highly praised *The Courage to Be* (Yale University Press, 1952), Klemm perceived history's opposition to myth, in which being equals history; nonbeing, the landscape. Tillich's idea of being versus nonbeing was coupled to the act of self-affirmation and creation by man, including his technology. Klemm writes, "This attitude—production is progress, progress exists for itself, man has ontic destiny—represents an obsession with history and seems like a justification of self-glorification on a historical plane by nations (as in the American attempt at genocide of the native Indians for reasons of progress and destiny) or by individuals (the reality-transforming assassination of Robert Kennedy)."

Noting Tillich's view that man is anxiously caught between history and nature as the common ground of history and existentialism, he perceives that the existentialist funk in absurdity and death is inextricably woven into the proud "courage to be in spite of nonbeing, for the sake of and by the grace of history." Contrasting this to the cosmogonic mythical mode as described by Mircea Eliade, Klemm notes that "the correlation of Being and History, as per Tillich, cuts man off from nature and the mystery of life. Modern culture has made that correlation and history becomes its 'ultimate concern.' " Klemm cites Eliade's comment that most men have no real role in history either. He quotes Eliade: "History either makes itself (as the result of the seed sown by acts that occurred in the past, several centuries or even millenia ago . . .) or it tends to be made by an increasingly smaller number of men who not only prohibit the mass of their contemporaries from directly or indirectly intervening in the history they are making, but in addition have at their disposal means sufficient to force each individual to endure, for his own part, the consequences of this history, that is to live immediately and continuously in dread of history." *Myth of the Eternal Return.* (New York: Harper, 1959.)

"The terror of history," Klemm concludes, "lies in the great destruction it has wrought on our planet and our people, and in the perversion of our natural religious sensitivities to place and the source of Life. We are left with the dull mentality of the competitive, acquisitive, contractual being whose essence is determined by the outcome of situations. Thought is consumed in the fearful expectancies of coming events, daily tedium, and sentimental recall of the past. As historical beings, we stand condemned by our history and are helpless in the face of it." In this connection, see also Kai Nielson, "On Taking Human Nature as the Basis of Morality," in John J. Mitchell, ed., *Human Nature: Theories, Conjectures, Descriptions* (New York: Metuchen, 1972).

10. Any number of Holy Land places are celebrated and are the goal of a passionate tourism. But this is largely literal, childish behavior in a religious view that celebrates nonplace. The forty years of Moses and the forty days of Jesus in the wilderness were consummated in a setting that was forever to do away with the centrality of nature, animals, art, and seasons. Even the betrothal between Jehova and Israel did not include a participatory role for nature—the promised land more a dowry than a member.

Humans being human, the tribes of neither Israel nor Judah could keep myth and ritual out, so that the woe and destruction of prophecy were directed about as much toward internal weakness and backsliding as toward enemy nations. Indeed, the rich poetic vision of the land in parts of the Old Testament overshadows the lean view of the prophets. It has been argued that the Old Testament is a nature-sensitive document (see, for example, Eric G. Freudenstein, "Ecology and the Jewish Tradition," *Judaism Magazine* 14, no. 4 [Fall 1970]). But the argument stands up only in contrast to other parts of the book—the "thou shalts" and the "thou shalt nots" directed toward duties in property, not beings. The celebration of natural beauty and the cautionary words against abuse of soil or livestock do not indicate appreciation of an independent reality so much as respect for providential mastery and rights in property; they are not an imputation of an ethical domain outside that of codes of ownership. It is, however, true, says Henri Frankfort (*Kingship and the Gods* [Chicago: University of Chicago Press, 1948], pp. 343–44), that much of the reference to nature in the Old Testament is poetic—in the modern sense of man "expressing his moods in its imagery . . . but never sharing its mysterious life, never an actor in the perennial cosmic pageant."

11. This distinction between practice and theory helps us to understand the consternation among Christians and Jews as to the responsibility of their respective religious views for the "environmental crisis." The ambiguity of Christian spokesmen on the responsibility of Christianity for the destruction of nature is an extraordinary example of the problem of just what "Christian" or "Jewish" means. Does one judge a religion by its orthodox position or by the culture of which it is part? Are what were once heretical views that were later incorporated part of the official church or not? Is the Manichaean thought of Augustine, for example, to be regarded as contrary to Christian teaching or as part of it? No doubt varying degrees of purist versus pluralist views exist within religions. As a nominal, "cultural" Christian, my feeling is that the dominant religion of a society is always in some degree responsible even for the ideas and behaviors of heretics and opponents because its collective perceptions and values are far broader and more general than its formal apparatus and heretics are usually believers who simply want to revise details.

12. *In Bluebeard's Castle* (New Haven: Yale University Press, 1971), pp. 37–41.

13. David Miller, *The New Polytheism* (New York: Harper & Row, 1974).

14. *The Ideological Imagination* (Chicago: Quadrangle, 1972). In describing the normal appearance of the fear of strangers in man and other animals, Gordon W. Bronson says that such aversive

reactions peak at about three months in the infant, then sub-
side. Psychiatric "problems," however, heighten this fear reaction and result in a continuing obsession with the familiar. I
conclude from this that a society in whose interest fear and
hostility toward strangers were desirable—as among the military, for example—would find means of tweaking mother-
infant relations so that such "psychiatric problems" occurred
("The Development of Fear in Man and Other Animals," *Child
Development* 39 no. 2 [June, 1968]. Erik H. Erikson sees this fear
of strangers (and strange animals and flora) as "the first fear of
alienation," the "dread of being left alone in a universe without
a supreme counterplayer," a mixing of anxiety and rage that
"persists into all later phases of life and can pervade a widening
range of relationships" (*Toys and Reasons* [New York: W. W.
Norton, 1977], p. 50). What better description could one ask of
the psychopathic basis of philosophical existentialism or simply
the frightening aloneness of modern mass man?

15. *Bird in the Bush* (New York: New Directions, 1959), p. 20.
16. Noting that Israel was only about one hundred by sixty miles,
    Watsuji Tetsuro observes: "That small tribe of Israel has
    forced Europeans to believe for over 2,000 years that the
    history of Israel, in fact, reads almost like that of the whole
    human species" (*Climate and Culture* [Hokuseido Press, 1961],
    p. 53). George Williams's *Wilderness and Paradise in Christian
    Thought* (New York: Harper & Row, 1962) is pertinent here, in
    terms of the European elaboration of metaphors of "desert,"
    "wilderness," "paradise," and so on. But a more literal trans-
    fer also took place. As temperate climate climaxes were broken
    by the march of civilization, they inevitably became slightly
    more xeric. Grasslands tended to become deserts and, indeed,
    to be called deserts from the first by Europeans (Martyn
    Bowden, "The Great American Desert," in Martyn Bowden
    and David Lowenthal, eds., *Geographies of the Mind* [New York:
    Oxford University Press, 1976]).
17. An excellent example of this is given by Richard Rabkin: "A
    curious natural phenomenon is the extended predator-victim
    relationships of distinct animal groups, such as that between
    hyenas and wildebeests. When a hyena pack picks off newborn
    wildebeests on the plains of Africa one option is to focus upon

the individuals involved. Under these circumstances, the hyena needs no introduction to us. He is the proverbial despicable coward who terrorizes the innocent and the weak. The mere sight of him arouses our dislike; his elimination is the strategy of choice. This conceptualization of events follows the linear or historical point of view.

"From another approach, this encounter can be said to have, at least, the virtues of being genuine and authentic. As such, we can appreciate that 'this is darkest Africa.' Such a jarring juxtaposition of views is hard to assimilate or translate into human interaction, although this has been done in literature. Thus, Norman Mailer has defended (infamously, it has been charged) the 'authenticity' of the juvenile delinquent's act of smashing an old storekeeper over the head with a gun. More abstractly, Camus' hero Meursault in *The Stranger* has an iconoclast's view of the individualistic position, and does not construct events in sequence but simply considers the raw facts; although in the novel he is judged in court as a born criminal type, Camus indicates that the former orientation has the virtues of genuineness and authenticity. This, in short, represents the 'time as a point' model.

"From a third point of view, the hyena's career is to be a scavenger; the natural history of his species inevitably leads to such behavior. Finally, adopting the fourth or cyclical viewpoint, there is a sudden expansion of focus. The hyena and wildebeest disappear as structures, as individuals. What is noteworthy in this context is a series of processes and their repetitions. There exist two systems, the wildebeest herd and the hyena pack, which repeatedly impinge on one another in a very special way. It becomes evident that the hyena pack lives in harmony with other systems such as the bird flock or the jackal pack, which also live together with it and the wildebeest herd. On reflection it becomes apparent that the elimination of hyenas would eliminate the wildebeests; the herd would overgrow its food supply, its composition would tend toward old, feeble, sick animals, disease would spread, and so forth. For the wildlife manager, the question becomes how many wildebeests the hyenas should be allowed to kill in order to keep the herd's composition at given proportions or size, for what desired outcome. The hyena is actually drawn to the newborn wildebeest because there have been many wildebeests calving at the same time in this location, and the smell of placental blood attracts him. In rather far-fetched teleological terms, he is drawn by the potential population explosion and the danger to the wildebeest herd.

"What starts out in the historical framework as a repellent situation involving the individual hyena and the newborn wildebeest becomes in this model a repetition, a cycle that has long endured. To save individual wildebeests may ultimately endanger the entire herd. This 'ecological consciousness,' as the conservationists call it, challenges much of Western political and religious philosophy" (*Inner and Outer Space* [New York: Norton, 1970], pp. 102–3).

18. A. Bouhdiba, "The Child and the Mother in Arab-Muslim Society," in L. Carl Brown and Norman Itzkowitz, eds. *Psychological Dimensions of Near Eastern Studies* (Princeton, N.J.: Darwin Press, 1977). In the same volume, psychiatric illness is rated at over 50 percent in a Lebanese village under study (compared with 80 percent in midtown Manhattan) (Herant Katchadourian, "Culture and Psychopathology," *ibid.*).

19. Rudolf Eckstein and Elaine Caruth, "From Eden to Utopia," *American Imago* 22 (1965): 1; pp. 128–141.

20. Following Arnold Van Gennep's *The Rites of Passage* (Chicago: University of Chicago Press, 1960), Eliade has carefully set out the initiatory sequence in its most widespread and general form: preparation of the sacred ground and isolation of the candidates, instruction of the novices, physical ceremonies (circumcision, tooth extraction), ritual pantomimes ("death," "rebirth"), and dietary and other prohibitions (*Rites and Symbols of Initiation* [New York: Harper & Bros., 1958] pp. 21–40). I believe that anyone reading the literature on the psychology of adolescence in Erikson, Anna Freud, Blos, Kiell, or others cannot help but be struck by the correlation of the social events under Eliade's "benign intercession of elders" with the psychological 'readiness' of the adolescent for the tests, special knowledge, new kinships, and the rites of expulsion, exile, and incorporation.

21. According to Jay Y. Gonen, patriarchal societies frustrate the

adolescent's transferral of his love of mother to others or to nature. This results in a massive repressed rage toward the father, especially among competing sons, a hatred that in turn incurs guilt. The harsh authoritarianism is intended to "control sexual love toward the mother." Tenderness is allowed but all expression of sensuality is redirected to prostitutes. The neurotic love of the adolescent therefore includes "an overwhelming desire to rescue the beloved." This seems to mean that a society that manipulates and destroys the natural world as though it were a woman in chattel will evoke a minority of antagonists bent on saving her, whose arguments will seem emotional, romantic, and immature to the more "realistic" majority. It would follow that the minority of "nature lovers" would be acting on a muted rage and that guilt over their hostility would make them seek punishment, perhaps from the dominant authorities or perhaps by a natural calamity. Presumably the sons of the patriarchs who are redirected toward prostitutes will perceive nature or some part of it as fallen, or undeserving of their tenderness, freeing them to exploit it for money with callous disregard for its own inner state or consequences. Both nature destruction and preservation can be interpreted in these terms as an unresolved oedipal problem—which is not an unexpected analysis if desert-mindedness is a destructuring of late childhood developmental processes (*A Psychohistory of Zionism* [New York: Mason/Charter, 1975], pp. 10, 12).

22. Edith Jacobson speaks of this "acting out" behavior as "unwillingness to accept and adjust to reality," a "global projection identification" in which external objects become unacceptable parts of the self, to be changed via political or legal means," an attitude leading toward "megalomaniac ideas" (*Psychotic Conflict and Reality* [New York: International Universities Press, 1967], pp. 19, 35, 59).

23. Ideologists tend toward totalism, says Gonen: "Persons with a negative identity . . . resort to a rigid ideology to achieve totality at the expense of wholeness" (*A Psychohistory of Zionism*, p. 309).

24. Tetsuro says of the desert peoples, "Man does not wait passively for nature's blessings; he makes active incursions into nature's domain and succeeds in snatching a meagre prey

from her. This fight with nature leads directly to a fight with the other man; it is like two sides of a coin—on the reverse side the fight with nature, the fight with man on the obverse." "The singularity of the desert forced the tribal god into a personal manlike mould. . . . God was the realization of the oneness of man in his struggle against nature, so there are here no marks of the deification of the forces of nature" (*Climate and Culture*, pp. 49, 55).

25. I conclude from this that the terrorist is the supreme revolutionary, who in turn is the extreme ideologist, all of them acting out their responses to "the demands of inner change" that normally revolutionize the self, but which may be impossible if they are trapped in an immature society. In totemic thought, the outer world is transformed metaphorically; in Neolithic thought, this metaphor was emphatically maternal; in Western thought, the metaphor is denied, leaving the adolescent to act on the literal-mindedness of his childhood and direct the transforming impulse to political ends. The work of the final phases of young-adult training in traditional societies is to temper the idealism that was so necessary as a bonding cement in its early phases. Transferred to ideological ends, that idealism appears to become inflamed and insatiable. The effect in the long run, says Steiner, is a loathing of an impossible goal, a desire for war "for the sake of identity," a "nostalgia for disaster." The need for rebirth is projected upon the world, so that it, rather than one's own childish self, is to be destroyed (*In Bluebeard's Castle*, p. 19). For the relationship of history, ideology, and totalitarianism, see Hannah Arendt, "Ideology and Terror, a Novel Form of Government," *Review of Politics* 15 [1953]: 303). Arendt holds that totalitarian thought of the past century finds intellectual support in the Darwinian theory of evolution and that violent revolution and tyranny are therefore presented as extensions of a "natural" process. In this, Arendt is insufficiently critical. Herbert Schneidau speaks more to the point when he says: "Western thinking is strange, aberrant, and requires arduous training"; "We have been misled by a spurious analogy with evolution and maturation into believing that ours is the 'normal' way to think" (*Sacred Discontent*, pp. 57, 58).

26. The similarity of modern Americans to drifting Bedouin

nomads is a penetrating criticism, the inferences of which for the study of Hebrews, and even Islam, will be lost only to theologians intent upon differentiations rather than similarities. Islam, or "submission," has perpetuated with gusto the tide of tawdry skirmishing that goes on endlessly in the Near Eastern desert. Its best description may still be Robert Doughty's *Deserta Arabia*—a hard-line, calculated balance of accommodation and hospitality motivated by suspicion and vengeance, loyalty and deception, the exaltation of will and honor, rituals of procedure, overdefined boundaries, overstructured sensory modes, fantasies of scheming enemies, fatalism, discipline, hierarchic relationships, goal-oriented behavior, anxiety, hostility, and despair. Islam, in its perpetual crises, dreams of extrication by a heroic outsider, a rescue, escape, or messiah—sharing this with older Arabic attitudes and the Hebrews, Jews, and Christians. Deliverance of this kind is premised on the model of centuries of equestrian strife and the unpredictable, calculating judgment of the worth of those in need of help from distant warlords or petty chiefs, who may or may not come to their aid.

27. Gonen discusses the psychological problems of a people without a place or home as centering on their loss of identity. To this they respond with the "hyper-vigilance of the haunted, the alert scanning of the insecure, and the continuous suspiciousness of the vulnerable" (*A Psychohistory of Zionism*, p. 32). See also Lewis H. Lapham, "The Melancholy Herd," Harper's, July, 1978.

28. M. von Senden, *Space and Sight* (London: Methuen, 1960).

29. This statement will no doubt be taken as an attack on Jewish mothers. I suspect that the literature on Jewish mothers by Jewish sons bears out an obsessive syndrome between them that may indeed be related to the theme of this essay. On the whole, however, I see the failure of nurturance among Jews, as among Christians and Muslims, as reflecting not one or the other of the parents, but rather the whole of the nurturing activity of society common to the Western experience. As for the fearful child shutting down because of a fearful mother, see Joseph Chilton Pearce, *Magical Child* (New York: Dutton, 1977), pp. 102–7.

4. The Puritans

1. A colleague and historian tells me that "the West" means Europe, not the Near East. But I am unable to understand the events of his West, even its Renaissance or industrial era, except as transformations of themes from the millennia of turmoil and religious conceptions east of the Mediterranean.
2. Joseph Campbell, *The Masks of God:* vol. 3, *Occidental Mythology* (New York: Viking, 1964), p. 267. The point here is that the "symbolizing" of an individual passage by natural phenomena, such as the death and birth of the seasons, is more than an analogical illustration; it frames the external event in implications carried over psychologically from the individual's inner experience. Such an experience is the linguistic, binary coding associated with the emergence of cognition in childhood. This order-giving classification by an either/or procedure is normal for the small child (see Eric Lenneberg, *Biological Foundations of Language* [New York: John Wiley and Sons, 1967, 326–335] and Frank Smith and George Miller, eds., *The Genesis of Language* [Cambridge: Massachusetts Institute of Technology Press, 1966]. Societies that use the same natural phenomena (such as plant and animal species) in their symbolizing counteract the fragmenting effects of taxonomy at a later life stage.
3. *Occidental Mythology*, p. 174.
4. But their rubric differs. While most see Western self-consciousness as dating from the second millennium B.C., it is not clear whether Judaic discontent and alienation, repeated social and civic disruption and disaster, the "challenge" of the environment, the mixing of cultures, or something else is behind it. One of the most novel theories is Julian Jaynes's speculation that, until that time, one side of the brain spoke to the other, telling it in an "audible" voice what to do, so that no one ever had to think out the next step or to reflect on himself as an independent will (*The Origins of Consciousness in the Breakdown of the Bicameral Mind* [Boston: Houghton-Mifflin, 1977]). Whatever one thinks of his theory, Jaynes's version at least has the virtue of insisting that the emergence of a Western consciousness must go beyond the events normally described in history and the ideological record. He accounts for the collapse of the

old dual system (in the tensions and anxieties of the times), especially the effects of being ruled by tyrants who invaded from the north.

5. Robert Persig, *Zen and the Art of Motorcycle Maintenance* (New York: Bantam Books, 1977). Persig's description of the eclipse of one side of Greek thought (pp. 350–85) is highly readable and interesting and helps to clarify the transition from the preclassical, earth-centered peoples who figure in the building and use of the ancient religious sites, so brilliantly described by Vincent Scully in *The Earth, the Temple, and the Gods* (New Haven: Yale University Press, 1962). The conventional view is one of Greeks before Homer, immersed in the great life-in-the-round, in which nature and human nature were celebrated inextricably in a numinous and spirit-filled world, while the later Greek demythologizing and life of the mind of the classical Greek writers is associated with the culmination of Athens. But the rationalistic, hierarchic thought of Hellenistic Greece may not have so dominated Greece as it did neoclassic thought in Europe after the thirteenth century. Even Aristotle does not fall neatly into the manipulative, man-centered view that gave rise to modern philosophy. John Rodman points out that in the works of Plato not emphasized by modern scholarship there exists a very different, more ecological Aristotle ("The Other Side of Ecology in Ancient Greece," *Inquiry* 18 [1976]: 115–25). In spite of the immense corpus of work on ancient Greece, very little has been directly addressed to their attitudes toward nature until recently. Clarence Glacken's *Traces on the Rhodian Shore* (Berkeley: University of California Press, 1967) was a major contribution. Pablo Vivante's *The Homeric Imagination* (Bloomington, Ind.: University of Indiana Press, 1970) is also very helpful.

6. The fear of machines is discussed in several places, notably in Hans Sachs, "The Delay of the Machine Age," *Psychoanalytic Quarterly* 2 (1933): 404 and in Ernst Hans Gombrich, *Caricature* (London: Phaidon, 1940). The psychoanalytic idea that the intimidating effect is due to a failure of metaphorical perception seems opposed to our sense of the Greeks as masters of adolescent initiation rites—ceremonies whose primary function was to foster mature perspective and just such analogical thought.

7. *Occidental Mythology*, p. 228. Homosexuals do protest that theirs is a "style" rather than a deformity of life. The male bond described by Lionel Tiger in *Men in Groups* (New York: Random House, 1969) does not itself imply a failure of development, but rather a stage of attachments projected forward in the life cycle from the juvenile fraternalism that has a special function in the band of adult male hunters. There is psychoanalytic evidence that homosexuality is often associated with psychopathology, especially manifested as identity problems. Perhaps the evolutionary scenario was the development of human ontogeny in which juvenile same-sex bonding was reconstituted in adults as a means of achieving goal-directed, cooperative effort, although its success depended on keeping overt sexuality apart. The love of the child for the parent of the opposite sex was perhaps an instrument for doing so, helping the child keep separate the same-sex bond from the eros of potential mate.

8. See particularly Rollo May, *Love and Will* (New York: Norton, 1969), pp. 280–95. Most important to the demythologizing was the marriage of Platonic idealism and the Hebrew heritage of purity striving. These are almost clinical expressions of the adolescent dreaming of perfection, just as a kind of jaded skepticism and anomie are typical of adult disillusionment where those normal idealisms are not transformed by mature resolution through a realistic acceptance of human limitations and affirmation of the naturalness and imperfection inherent in the human condition.

9. Among modern writers, the most enthusiastic espouser of this holistic trend in medieval Christianity is C. S. Lewis (*Studies in Medieval and Renaissance Literature* [Cambridge, 1966]; *The Discarded Image* [Cambridge, 1964]). For the historical description, see Jean Seznec, *Survival of the Pagan Gods* (Princeton, N.J.: Princeton University Press, 1953).

10. There are so many sources on the widely recognized efflorescence of the twelfth and thirteenth centuries that it is difficult to pick a representative historical overview. Perhaps the resurgence of the feminine epitomizes it, as described in C. S. Lewis's *The Allegory of Love* (Oxford University Press, 1936). The burst of biology as ecstatic taxonomic peripeteia, exemplified by Konrad von Gesner, and the refurbishment of her-

bals, the plants drawn from life instead of copied from old herbals, did not grow out of the physical-mathematical sciences as did the rest of pre-Darwinian biology but were, in fact, suppressed by them (Charles E. Raven, *Natural Religion and Christian Theology* [Cambridge, 1953]; Otto Pacht, "Early Italian Nature Studies and the Early Calendar Landscape," *Journal of the Warburg and Courtauld Institutes* 13, nos. 1–2 [1950], pp. 13–46).

11. Lewis, *The Discarded Image*, p. 146.

12. Barfield, Owen *Saving the Appearances* (London: Faber and Faber, 1957), p. 109.

13. Because of their rejection of bodily symbols, ecologizing Protestant Christian spokesmen are in a bind. Those syncretic figures that best represent the organic continuum are the result of ten centuries of compromise with pagan cultures. So they must pick and choose instead from biblical passages exhorting man's stewardship of the earth or cite those saints who display compassion for or the utility of nature, like Francis of Assisi, Benedict, or Ambrose.

14. For a description of Dante's ecology, see Joseph Meeker, *The Comedy of Survival* (Los Angeles: Guild of Tutors Press, 1980).

15. The Protestants' resources for formulating dualism were greater, in terms of cumulative historical and ideological precedent, than were those of their puritan models. These resources have been called euphemistically "the sources of Christian asceticism." They include Paul's Greek Mithraism— the notion that the world is the site of a titanic conflict between the followers of Christ and those of Satan; Greek cults of continence; late Judaism's sense of sexuality as impure; Orphism's view of the body as a drag on the soul; Essene war with the world; apocalyptic martyrdom—"the ecstatic and pneumatic Christ-possessed personality with its glorying in suffering"; Tertullian; Clement; Origen . . . the list goes on and on. It is as though there were something at work in the new critical self-consciousness itself that generated disgust with the body and the natural, perhaps as a defense against the loss of connectedness with the ecological systems upon which one is dependent (Marvin Monroe Deems, "The Sources of Christian Asceticism," in John Thomas McNeil, Matthew Spinks, and

Harold R. Willoughby, eds., *Environmental Factors in Christian History* [Chicago: University of Chicago Press, 1939]).

As for Paul, he is sometimes presented as a sort of ecologist because he is so eloquent on the Incarnation. Theologians tend to see in it a transcendence of the duality of spirit and body. But the Christians have debated the meaning and ambiguity of the Incarnation for a millennium and a half. To a nontheologian, the dual existence of Christ as man and God does not prove the sacred integration of the natural and spiritual, but is instead a temporary amalgam, a stamp of approval perhaps, revealing the hopelessness of the task of perceiving a basically dual system as a unity.

E. M. Cioran calls Paul a ranting, blue-nose shouter who seems furthest from patron sainthood of the environment— noisy, humorless, vengeful, a hater of solitude, of understanding, and of the sort of patient waiting and listening the naturalist needs in order to be touched by a continuity with the nonhuman world ("Two Portraits Retouched," *Second Coming Magazine*, July 1961, pp. 12–13).

16. The perceptual revolution associated with the mathematical measurement of space, especially as it was employed by Renaissance painters, is a familiar theme in the history of art (John White, *The Birth and Rebirth of Pictorial Space* [London: Faber and Faber, 1957]). As for its broader implications, the idea con brio is the subject of Marshall McLuhan and Harley Parker's *Through the Vanishing Point* (New York: Harper & Row, 1968). Awareness that Roman painting of the fourth century was also "in perspective" helps us to resist claiming too much or seeing it as another "consciousness revolution." To appreciate the reason it became so important in the modern world, one should read Christopher Hussy's *The Picturesque* (New York: Putnam's, 1927) and Elizabeth Manwaring's *Landscape in Eighteenth Century England* (New York: Oxford University Press, 1925), wherein we realize that generalizing of the spectatorship to which the observer is compelled by such separation and distancing evolved in the seventeenth and eighteenth century to tourism and connoisseurship and finally saturated education and entertainment by pictorializing. This matter of the disconnected observer, so clearly bound up with the genesis

of Renaissance painting, seems to me a return to Christian asceticism. Joseph Campbell says, "The orthodox Christian notion that nature is corrupt" is "an extreme statement of the implications of the Jewish myth of God apart from the world, creating, judging, condemning it, and then offering, as though from the outside, to endow some particle of its immensity with the virtue of his particular attention—as by a Covenant, Koran or Incarnation" (*Occidental Mythology*, p. 516). If you substitute "man the connoisseur" for "God" it appears that humanism, although it made a radical replacement of God by man, was very conventional in applying the same old Western sense of a divided creation.

17. To be out of *touch* with your own body is to be unable to *feel* its separation from the environment. "Global projection" identifications are typical of young children and psychotic adults who "turn external objects into intolerable or desirable but unacceptable parts of his own self," says Edith Jacobson (*Psychotic Conflict and Reality* ([New York: International Universities Press, 1967], p. 35.) Early "maternal mismanagement of touch," says Anthony Storr, makes the individual distrustful of his own body and senses, creating later problems of *feeling* for the outer world, not only in terms of unfeelingness, but of chaotic impressions (*The Dynamics of Creation* [New York: Atheneum, 1972], p. 64).

18. R. E. Money-Kryle, *Man's Picture of His World* (London: Duckworth, 1968), pp. 45–55.

19. Peter Blos, "The Second Individuation Process of Adolescence," *The Psychoanalytic Study of the Child*, vol. 22, 1967, pp. 163–186. I suspect that much of modern society finds it difficult to believe that "we" are such haters and destroyers of the natural world—there is so much evidence in our daily lives to the contrary: all this attention to the environment! But the point is exactly as Blos says: one clings as one despises. Denial of the importance of the nonhuman environment, says Harold Searles, leads to overdependence on it (*The Nonhuman Environment* [New York: International Universities Press, 1960] p. 395). It is the trap that dualism sets for itself: Luther's obsession with feces and the devil, which are anathema to him, as opposed to the vulgar patriarchy of the twentieth century

(Philip Wylie, *Generation of Vipers* [New York: Farrar & Rinehart, 1942], chapter 11; Aldous Huxley, "Mother," *Tomorrow and Tomorrow and Tomorrow*, pp. 172–83), the avid animal protectionists in a world of slaughter houses, and so on. Ironically enough, the spokesmen of institutionalized and corporate progress (e.g., land-skinning maximizers of wheat, cotton, oil, timber, etc.) exploit this psychic twitch to prove that "we" are actually conservers. The genesis of this twitch is in the style with which the culture programs individual nurturing: inadequate symbiosis precedes inevitable separation. The experience of separateness is born deformed, and one cannot forgive (or forget) the other for splitting off "too soon."

20. A sometimes overlooked but excellent study of the dynamic interrelationship of the holy family as a model of coherence for Christians, with the rising importance of the Madonna during the Dark Ages, then her eclipse by the Protestant patriarchy, and its symbolism in the masculine lines of elm trees of "Yankee City" as opposed to the virgin wilderness, is W. Lloyd Warner's *The Living and the Dead* (New Haven, 1959), pp. 46–49.

21. The most pithy statement on this is David Crownfeld's "The Curse of Abel," *North American Review*, Summer 1973. For a more explicitly Freudian description of the anal fixation and its effect on world view, see Norman O. Brown, *Life Against Death* (Middletown, Conn.: Wesleyan University Press, 1959), pp. 179–210.

22. Jurus G. Draguns, "Values Reflected in Psychopathology: The Case of the Protestant Ethic," *Ethos* 2, no. 2 (1974), pp. 115–136. Philip J. Greven, Jr., in *The Protestant Temperament* (New York: Alfred Knopf, 1977), has examined hostility to the self and body as central to American evangelical puritanism. The autonomous body functions are always a threat to systems of self-control, which are first inculcated in the child by external authority. The guilt and shame that make up so much of the Protestant conscience are based on the association of those uncontrollable (or animalistic or satanic) sexual and excretory functions—indeed, all spontaneous emotions—with corruption and sin. Born-again Christians, he says, are locked into "profound alienation of the individuals from their own bod-

ies" (p. 65), in "sustained hostility toward the body and all its manifestations and demands" (p. 66). The body is the daily, inescapable experience of the world's corruption, and the most a puritan could hope for in this life was dissociation from his own body, a "quest for nothingness" (p. 82), in which the most powerful desire is a loss of self-identity. Ideally, a child reared among the evangelicals was totally obedient by the age of two. "Break their wills that you may spare their souls," directed John Wesley (p. 35). A metaphor used by Anne Bradstreet is interesting, relating body and nature: "Some children (like sowre land) are so tough and morose a disposition, that the plough of correction must make long furrows on their back, and the Harrow of discipline goe often over them before they bee fit soile to sow the seed of morality, much less of grace in them" (p. 49).

23. Quoted in Perry Miller, *The New England Mind* (New York: Macmillan, 1939), p. 208.
24. Jonathan Edwards, ed., *Images or Shadows of Divine Things*, by Perry Miller (New Haven: Yale University Press, 1948).
25. The desert origin of the puritan ambivalence can also be seen in the attitudes of Arab Muslims toward the feminine and women. On the one hand they are almost totally derealized, on the other sentimentally idealized (A. Bouhdiba, "The Child and the Mother in Arab-Muslim Society," in L. Carl Brown and Norman Itzkowitz, eds., *Psychological Dimensions of Near Eastern Studies* [Princeton, N.J.: Darwin Press, 1977]).
26. Charles L. Sanford, *The Quest for Paradise* (Urbana, Ill.: University of Illinois Press, 1961). To recapitulate: all adolescents are given to dreaming about a perfect world, which projects the desire for the imminent improvement in themselves upon the world. Since their own psychological transformation is preceded by a "programmed personality dissolution," the projection bears this destructive requirement as that impulse is expressed in mythical and ideological thought. In the first it is often implicit in the cycle of the seasons and the rituals of sacrifice, while in the second it can be caught up as the justification of no end of horrors. From its start, Christianity has fostered the view that the world was about to end, but I think this can be too easily interpreted as eschatological rather than psychological.

27. Paul Shepard, *Man in the Landscape* (New York: Knopf, 1967); Bernard Smith, *European Vision and the South Pacific* (London: Oxford University Press, 1960).

28. Sigmund Freud believed, for example, that the psychical foundation of all travel was the first separation and the various other departures from one's mother, including the final journey into death. Journeying is therefore an activity related to a larger feminine realm, so that it is not surprising that Freud himself was ambivalent about it. Of the landscape he said, "All of these dark woods, narrow defiles, high grounds and deep penetrations are unconscious sexual imagery, and we are exploring a woman's body." "I am a conquistadore!" The pleasure of travel he believed to be rooted in the fulfillment of early wishes, that is, successful mastery of the body—one's own and the maternal. Of course, departures and passages are the essential fulcrum of maturing processes, provided we are transformed. Everything depends on what happens at the end (Leonard Shengold, "The Metaphor of the Journey in 'The Interpretation of Dreams,' " *American Imago* 23, (Winter 1966): 4, pp. 287–315.

29. See Mircea Eliade, *The Quest* (Chicago: University of Chicago Press, 1969), pp. 90–126.

30. Mircea Eliade, "The Nostalgia for Paradise in Primitive Tradition," *Myths, Dreams and Mysteries* (New York: Harper, 1970); Howard Rollin Patch, *The Other World According to Descriptions in Medieval Literature* (Cambridge, 1950), and his "The Yearning for Paradise in Primitive Tradition," *Diogenes*, Summer, 1953, pp. 18–30.

31. Rudolf Eckstein and Elaine Caruth, "From Eden to Utopia," *American Imago* 22 (1965): 128. The problem with all utopias, Eckstein and Caruth say, is the inevitable intrusion of reality. For the individual, this accompanies the first eruption of teeth, nipple biting, and weaning (or expulsion from the garden). The myth of paradise is a fantasy that helps one bear the frustration of that loss and incorporates enough reality to serve "to defend against the resurgence of the earlier, uninhibited fantasy" and modify it as an acceptable ideal.

32. Deferred gratification is one of those psychological-jargon phrases in everyday use. The convention holds that the infant and child simply learn to wait for what they want and to resist

a fantasized substitute, and that thereafter such realistic patience is a measure of maturity. Ethologically the matter is more interesting, since a great many kinds of vertebrate animals often defer to more powerful competitors. This is especially true of hierarchically organized social carnivores and primates. Clearly, deferred gratification is not the product of unique human reason at all, but a widespread form of animal behavior, and, in us, is probably a legacy from our animal heritage. Its failure or breakdown may indeed be immature, but is symptomatic of behavioral pathologies more complex than rational understanding or educational failure. The modern appetite for change defines protean man.

5.   The Mechanists

1. John B. Calhoun, "Environmental Control over Four Major Paths of Mammalian Evolution," in J. M. Thoday and A. S. Park, eds., *Genetic and Environmental Influences on Behavior* (New York: Plenum, 1968).
2. Claire and William S. Russell, "The Sardine Syndrome," *The Ecologist* 1, no. 2 (August 1970).
3. Garrett Hardin, "Nobody Ever Dies of Overpopulation." *Science* 171: 527, 1971.
4. Stephen Boyden, "Biological View of Problems of Urban Health," *Human Biology in Oceania* 1, no. 3 (February 1972). Boyden calls this the "principle of phylogenetic maladjustment." He emphasizes that much of this maladjustment is chronic, mild, and difficult to diagnose. He sees three major aspects: crowding and the rapid evolution of parasitic viruses; physical debility due to inadequate exercise and the effects of drugs, alcohol, and tobacco; and the chemicalization of the environment by the introduction of more than ten thousand new compounds per year, many of which have possible psychological as well as physiological effects.
5. Robert Browning, "Up at a Villa—Down in the City," *Complete Poetic and Dramatic Works* (New York: Houghton Mifflin, 1895).
6. Patricia Draper, "Crowding Among Hunter-Gatherers: The !Kung Bushmen," *Science* 182 (1973): 301.

7. For differences in "interpersonal press" in persons per room as opposed to buildings per acre, see Omer R. Galle, Walter R. Gove, and J. Miller McPherson, "Population Density and Pathology: What Are the Relations for Man?" *Science* 176 (1972): 23–30. Although I have criticized its picky subdivisions, the article supports the thesis that city life increases psychiatric disorders and interferes with individual growth and development.

8. David E. Davis, in A. H. Esser, *Behavior and Environment* (New York: Plenum, 1971), p. 133. Jonathan L. Freedman, in *Crowding and Behavior* (New York: Viking, 1975), says that "feeling crowded" is subjective, hence is unrelated to actual density (p. 93); and a further bandying of words: While there is "no relation between crowding and pathology, . . . having to interact or deal with large numbers of people generally seems to have negative effects" (pp. 103, 123).

    There is much evidence on the relationship of density, stress, and their chain of effects on the immune system, the production of cortisone and lactic acid, calcium levels, adrenaline, and every aspect of human life-cycle behavior. Some of these factors are reviewed in Galle, Gore, and McPherson, "Population Density and Pathology," p. 23. The only explanation I can imagine for the continued publication of books and papers claiming that there are no detrimental effects of population density on human well-being, by writers who are apparently sincere, is the structure of the modern university, which rewards all publication, and the nature of modern statistical evidence, which enables an author to support any hypothesis depending on how the "problem" is stated. Moreover, such argle-bargle is congenial to an audience seeking evidence in support of a doctrine.

9. Paul D. MacLean, "The Paranoid Streak in Man," in Arthur Koestler and J. R. Smythes, eds., *Beyond Reductionism* (Boston: Beacon, 1968). The theory is that the limbic system (parts of the nervous system associated with emotional response to external signals) is triggered independently of higher mentation; yet those emotions need explanation and arouse irrational thought. "The paranoid demon" is "a general affect characterized as an unpleasant feeling of fear attached to something

that cannot be clearly identified," but which is "explained away." This response is based on the composite of reptilian, old mammalian, and new mammalian brains in the human head and leads to group exploitation of such widespread uneasiness by ideology. The authors suggest that the cause of such general nagging feelings may be the effects of overpopulation, especially the spatial squeeze and loss of personal identity.

10. I am aware of the supposed recovery potential of individuals to early brain damage, but the evidence is usually supported by rather minimal self-care criteria. The ideology of human independence from biological constraints is usually evident.

11. *Adolescence* (New York: D. Appleton & Co., 1904), pp. 229–31. Hall also lashes out against nomenclature and morphology as tedious substitutes for life history and evolutionary studies. He is right for the wrong reason. These subjects are inappropriate for the adolescent, who is characteristically interested in synthesis and process. Naming and structure are appropriate for the juvenile. Our error in education is to present the high school or college student with a whole package of biology as though all aspects of nature were suitable for his stage.

    The "typical textbook" referred to earlier is an otherwise excellent manual: Howard Gardener, *Developmental Psychology: An Introduction* (Boston: Little, Brown, 1978).

12. "The Experience of Living in Cities," *Science*, 13 March 1970, p. 167: 1461.

13. "A Strategy for the War with Nature," *Saturday Review*, 5 February 1966.

14. Karen Horney describes the quest for power and possessions as a form of protection against the feelings of helplessness and insignificance. Its satisfactions are without enduring enjoyment, for life is seen as an ordeal, its delays intolerable. Linked to implacable anxieties from infancy, it plays out "solutions" that cannot solve the problem (*The Neurotic Personality of Our Time* [New York: W. W. Norton, 1937], p. 166). A juvenile expression of the infantile fantasy of omnipotence is magic. It embodies the unlimited capacity to destroy (or cause to vanish) and to create—to bring into existence from nowhere. This connection is traced out in Arnold Modell's *Object Love and*

Reality (New York: International Universities Press, 1968) p. 168. To spring from nowhere and to disappear into nowhere suggest a world without transitions, that is, with faulty connections. Modell (pp. 28–40) and others have discussed the "transitional object"—such as the child's favorite blanket or toy—as an object to fill the gap between the self and the Other, a growing sense of separateness inadequately shielded by a parallel awareness of relationship. It could easily be assumed by a reader of that psychiatric literature that such a "security blanket" is normal for three-year-olds. But the children of Australian aborigines living in the bush do not cling to such objects and apparently do not need them. (Fred Myers, personal communication, May, 1981). I conclude from this that the transitional object in modern urban children is an early sign of the stresses within a culture centered on linear and broken, rather than holistic and integrative, patterns of reality. To speculate a step further, one may wonder to what degree such objects may become fixated on, as in a lifelong teddy-bear syndrome, and, indeed, whether the perpetuation into adult life of this form of dependence does not take on many shapes. To love another fully, says Modell, one must accept the separateness of objects and receive information about them from them (p. 61). The persisting transitional object expresses an infantile fear of identity in general and blocks recognition of true separateness or otherness by perceiving a representative object in a vague, comforting, omnipotent merging.

15. Anthony Storr (*The Dynamic of Creation* [New York: Atheneum, 1972] p. 177) notes that the breakdown of metaphor is characteristic of schizophrenia. This literalness or concreteness of perception grows from an *inadequate* separation of self and world. This seems odd, as we think of schizoid as a split that divides. But the contradiction is not real, for it is the terror of separateness that is at work. If the infant does not have a confident relationship with its mother, it cannot begin to separate from her, to take its first steps toward selfhood. As the growth calendar impels it into the arena of wider relationships, especially with the nonhuman world, the clinging identity-with continues its stranglehold. Freud described this peculiar fear as "uncanniness." Harold Searles (*The Nonhuman Environment*,

New York: I.U.P., 1960. pp. 174–177) has noted that recovery from acute schizophrenia is marked by the patient's ability to cope with strangers, strange places, and novel things. Compassion for the nonhuman arises from a sense of a shared situation in the universe. Paul Santmire puts the same duality somewhat differently. The division is between those who "flee" to the wilderness—a paganistic regression or fear of the future—and those who employ the "freedom of historical experience" against nature by dominating and destroying it—hence the "cults of rusticity and manipulation." Like the Russells, he sees the cultists as the psychological results of insecurity. Santmire, however, seeks the solution within Christianity, diagnosing the difficulty as "a failure to meet the challenge of historical experience"—that is, the acceptance of a God-given stewardship over the earth (*Brother Earth* [New York: Thomas Nelson, 1970] pp. 50–58).

16. *The Ideological Imagination* (Chicago: Quadrangle, 1972, p. 125). The full expression of ideological thinking—although it began with the pastoral philosophy of mounted tribes and the Hebrew pseudopastoralists of the Old Testament—is in the secular urban society: minimal enculturated religious conviction, maximum extension of pubertal abstract idealizing, and that "grazing posture" or provisional commitment to policy. Hannah Arendt observed the connection between this kind of puerility and terrorism ("Ideology and Terror: A Novel Form of Government," *Review of Politics* 15 [1953]: 303–27). Ideological thought is also at the root of all phrasing of man-nature relationships as alternatives. In this connection I prize D. H. Lawrence's remarks on the ideologists: "They are simply eaten up with caring. They are so busy caring about fascism or the League of Nations or whether France is right or whether marriage is threatened, that they never know where they are. They inhabit abstract space, the desert void of politics, principles, right and wrong" (quoted by Aldous Huxley, "D. H. Lawrence," *Collected Essays* [New York: Harper & Bros., 1959]). As for the "grazing posture" of contemporary life, see Lewis H. Lapham, "The Melancholy Herd," *Harper's*, July 1978, pp. 11–13.

17. This is the theme of Joseph Chilton Pearce's *Magical Child* (New York: Dutton, 1977).

18. Of this machine environment, Harold F. Searles says, "Over recent decades we have come from dwelling in an outer world in which the living works of nature either predominated or were near at hand, to dwelling in an environment dominated by a technology which is wondrously powerful and yet nonetheless dead, inanimate. I suggest that in the process we have come from being subjectively differentiated from, and in meaningful kinship with, the outer world, to finding this technology-dominated world an alien, so complex, so awesome, and so overwhelming that we have been able to cope with it only by regressing, in our unconscious experience of it, largely to a degraded state of nondifferentiation from it. I suggest, that is, that this 'outer' reality is psychologically as much a part of us as its poisonous waste products are part of our physical selves" ("Unconscious Processes in Relation to the Environmental Crisis," *Psychoanalytic Review* 59 [1972]: 361).

19. The attempt to change the world to meet one's own needs without reference to a "reality principle" is described as psychotic by Edith Jacobson in *Psychotic Conflict and Reality* (New York: International Universities Press, 1967), p. 18. What psychiatrists tend to mean by "reality" are the rather mundane things, such as not being able to change things by wishing. But if you conceive of reality in a Newtonian physical-chemical-energetic flux, reality is reduced to stuff; the psychiatrists' reality of forms and weights and size and doorways and being there and not being there vanishes, and "everything" becomes possible. The megalomania for deconstructing the planet earth is supported by the logic of such abstract "reality" and the "necessity" of "conquering nature." The most widely celebrated contemporary view that the world is a machine can be found in the works of Buckminster Fuller. Perhaps his penultimate statement is that we are a space colony on a "mother ship," that all biology is technology, and that "the universe is *nothing but* technology" ("Worlds Beyond," *Omni,* January 1979).

20. The "mechanistic world picture" is a Renaissance idea, Enlightenment theme, and industrial ethos. One of the characteristics of such a view is that we ourselves are, like the solar system or the atom, a kind of machine. The behavior of stressed and caged people, like that of other animals, has

always resulted in swaying, rocking, stereotyped movements, but as an active psychological model it was enormously stimulated by the environment of machines. The psychotic child who imitates machines is not unusual in the medical literature and shows that, in certain situations, a machine can be incorporated into the process in which the child internalizes aspects of external "beings" in the construction of a self.

Persig, in the most interesting part of his novel *Zen and the Art of Motorcycle Maintenance* (New York: Bantam Books, 1977), claims that the mechanistic model of life is derived from Aristotle's "dessicating, eyeless voice of dualistic reason" and Platonic idealism. The Sophists lost out, with their view of man as participant rather than observer (pp. 345–75). John Rodman believes that the alternative to the Aristotelian-Platonic core of modern self-consciousness was Empedoclean and Pythagorean ("The Other Side of Ecology in Ancient Greece," *Inquiry* 18 [1976]; 115–25). Others, like Jane Ellen Harrison, describe the division as between Olympian or classical, as opposed to Homeric or preclassical (*Mythology* [Boston: Marshall Jones, 1924]), or as Ionian cosmology versus "polytheistic liveliness" (David Miller, *The New Polytheism* [New York: Harper, 1974]). Perhaps these are merely different views of the same phenomenon, but it should be added that the matter was largely theoretical until Thomas Aquinas and others selectively rediscovered Greek thought—preferring those parts consistent with Christian abstraction and dualism—and the Renaissance mechanists and inventors created the means of acting upon it. My colleague James Bogen objects, with some justification, to blaming Plato for what the Protestant ethic and modern technicity have wrought. Yet, if one is to play the game of antecedence of modern ideas, ninety cents of the buck will stop with Plato and Aristotle.

21. A central thrust of puritan thought is the fallen or chaotic state of the world and its disgusting livingness—its quivering, pulsating, wet physiology. The fear of chaos, says Anthony Storr, is actually the fear of an *inner* disorder. It is a defense against the schizoid or depressive state, impulsive control, driven by disgust with spontaneous bodily functions. Out of it grows excessive attention to external precision and cleanliness,

highly useful in an electronic, sanitized world (*The Dynamics of Creation* [New York: Atheneum, 1972], pp. 92–98).

22. Such images do play a role in normal development, but not as an end in themselves. In all totemic societies, and probably in the evolution of art, these man-made images of nature serve as a kind of transitional object, midway, as Levi-Strauss says in *The Savage Mind* (Chicago: University of Chicago Press, 1962, pp. 1–34) between percepts and concepts. In his study of transitional objects, Arnold Modell has made it clear that such objects serve as a transient link between the psychological need to create an environment and the necessity of discovering the environment, reconciling the two. This gently guides the individual away from fantasies of omnipotence and anxieties of separation toward a love affair with the world (*Object Love and Reality*). The idea that art has its own ends has come into its own with the Renaissance. This independence of the most powerful tool of human imagination from the fostering of a unifying cosmology is one of the major features of the urban mind and helps distinguish the postindustrial city from all ancient cities. It also helps us to understand the frantic pursuit of "culture" by educated people, who experience the ambiguity and frustrations of its esthetic satisfactions on the one hand, and its isolating effects on the other.

    In spite of what I have said, I also recognize that participation in any art may have value for the individual as a creative way of resolving tensions and giving access to the unconscious so as to reduce the effects of repression (Storr, *The Dynamics of Creation*, p. 236–39).

23. In my view, Steiner's *In Bluebeard's Castle* (New Haven: Yale University Press, 1971), is the best book on human ecology of the twentieth century, although it is not ostensibly on man's relationship to nature at all. Read in that context it conveys a sense of an immense mindless yearning for destruction that is irresistible and inevitable. Like other literati, he speaks of the "dehumanizing" effects of the assembly line, the "bland mendacity" of the money market, and the massacres of 1915–1945, but I believe he is describing a desperate, profoundly human hysteria in the face of the accumulations of history and civilization. When we finally achieved the demythologized and desa-

cralized world extolled by the Hebrew-Christian-Muslim puritans, "control" over all the plants and animals—which was perfected in domestication, the final repudiation of everything organic in the very structure of our built environments—we reacted with the utmost material violence, not because of some failure to contain anarchic impulse, but because the humanism of literature and history is so discordant with the kind of being we are.

24. Harold F. Searles has observed that schizoid disorientation—the confusion of the sick individual as to where he is at any moment—would be tolerable to Hebrews in the desert, as it would to the rank and file in an army or a modern person in an underground train or in a jet aircraft. Perhaps this is the "homogenized" landscape against whose lack of orientation Eliade speaks of the necessity of sacred places or, again, the earthly home that to puritan thought is alien ("Non-differentiation of Ego Functioning in the Borderline Individual and Its Effect Upon His Sense of Personal Identity," paper presented at Sixth International Symposium on the Psychotherapy of Schizophrenia, Lausanne, Switzerland, Sept. 28, 1978; "A Case of Borderline Thought Disorder," *International Journal of Psycho-Analysis* 50 [1969]: 655.)

25. The tendency of the modern city—and agribusiness countryside—to become more uniform, as centralized mass production standardizes construction and land use, seems at first glance to be a side effect of progress, lamented by many. But is it only a by-product? If the general effect of urban life is to aggravate our sense of estrangement and our schizoid fears of the Other, such homogenization may soothe the harried psyche. Ask yourself whether, having traveled for weeks in a foreign land, you are not delighted to run across a motel or restaurant belonging to a familiar chain. If the world appears increasingly ominous and gloomy, as J. H. Van Den Berg says it does in "a defective state of mind" (*A Different Existence* [Pittsburg, Pa.: Duquesne University Press, 1972], pp. 8–9), then perhaps we react by trying to make it more familiar.

Can we experience both the denial of the nature of the outer world and an exaggerated sense of responsibility for it? The connection is a weak identity structure that cannot cope with one's own malevolence and a poor differentiation between inner and outer in which one projects feelings of help-lessness onto the outer world. The first results in the illusion of the peaceable kingdom, denying the reality of predation (or self aggression), the second in a sense of guilt for all the "badness" in the world. Some of us conservationists and environmentalists are uncomfortably close in our more excessive expressions of the world's decay and our more pastoral notions of how things should be.

6. The Dance of Neoteny and Ontogeny

1. Kenneth Keniston says, "The *extent* of human development is dependent upon the bio-social-historical matrix within which the child grows up; some developmental matrices may demonstrably retard, slow, or stop development; others may speed, accelerate, or stimulate it. . . . Human development is a very rough road, pitted with obstructions, interspersed with blind alleys, and dotted with seductive stopping places. It can be traversed only with the greatest of support and under the most optimal conditions" ("Psychological Development and Historical Change," in Robert Jay Lifton, ed., *Explorations in Psychohistory* [New York: Simon & Schuster, 1974], p. 149–64).
2. The infantilizing effect of domestication on animals has other effects far beyond the animals. Being incorporated into the human social system as its lowest-ranking members, their subservience becomes a kind of object lesson teaching a hierarchic scale of authority and right. Toward the animals themselves, the human feeling for their otherness evaporates in material values and sentimental affiliation. See Calvin Martin, "Subarctic Indians and Wildlife," in Carol M. Judd and Arthur J. Rays, eds., *Old Trails and New Directions: Papers of the Third North American Fur Trade Conference* (Toronto: University of Toronto, 1980).
3. Daphne Prior, "State of Surrender," *The Sciences.*
4. *The Time Falling Bodies Take to Light* (New York: St. Martin's Press, 1981). See his concept of enantiodromia, p. 131.
5. *Countertransference* (New York: International Universities Press, 1979), p. 175.
6. The fear of strangers in the child peaks at about three months,

then subsides. But defective nurturing heightens this reaction and perpetuates it as an obsession for the familiar (Gordon W. Bronson, "The Development of Fear in Man and Other Animals," *Child Development* 39, no. 2 [June 1968]). Erik Erikson sees this fear of strangers (and strange animals and flora) as "the first fear of alienation," the "dread of being left alone in a universe without a supreme counterplayer," a mixing of anxiety and rage that "persists into all later phases of life and can pervade a widening range of relationships" (*Toys and Reasons* [New York: W. W. Norton, 1977] p. 50).

7. Erik H. Erikson, "Play and Actuality," in Robert Jay Lifton and Eric Olson, eds., *Explorations in Psychohistory* (New York: Simon & Schuster, 1974).

8. In describing childhood thought as "iconic representation" (as opposed to infantile "sensory motor" perception or "acting out"), Jerome Bruner notes that children vary in their capacity for imagery, commenting that those with "low imagery" tend to replace it with language. These latter, "intellectually more supple," are held to have superior powers of conceptualization, but a "conventionalized memory," and lose the ability to preserve the distinctive quality of perceptual experience (*Studies in Cognitive Growth* [New York: John Wiley] pp. 21–28). It seems likely that such individuals (or such behavior) and their literary emphasis would be favored in societies rejecting icons and leaping forward to the symbolism of the printed word.

9. Much of the loneliness, sense of isolation, fragmentation, and crises of alienation of modern people—and, to some degree, the loss of "meaning" in their lives—is due to the collapse or subversion of Eliade's "maturational psychodynamics of adolescence." Erik Erikson describes it as "a loss of things to be true to," malfunctions of identity psychology, avoidance of commitment, the denial of ancestors and repudiation of the significance of the past, hypermobility, and excessive abstract idealism ("Youth, Fidelity and Diversity," in Alvin E. Winder and David L. Angus, eds., *Adolescence: Contemporary Studies* [New York: American Book Company, 1968] pp. 1–28, and Joseph L. Henderson, *Thresholds of Initiation* [Middletown: Wesleyan University Press, 1967]).

10. The term "inclusionist" is used here following Frederick Elder, who has described environmental attitudes as styles of inclusionist (seeing the world as a single reality) and exclusionist (believing that spiritual and human interests are independent of the natural realm) thought. See *Crisis in Eden* (New York: Abingdon Press, 1970), pp. 14–18.

11. The fanatic anality of Protestantism and capitalism has been fully discussed in Norman O. Brown's *Life Against Death* (Middletown, Conn.: Wesleyan University Press, 1959), p. 230. The Reformation, he says, was not due to toilet training but was "an eruption of fresh material from deeper strata of the unconscious, made possible by a large-scale transformation in the structure of the projective system (the culture). The dynamic of history is the slow return of the repressed" (p. 230).

12. *The Universal Experience of Adolescence* (New York: International Universities Press, 1964).

13. Joseph Chilton Pearce, *Magical Child* (New York: Dutton, 1977), pp. 45–50, 56–60.

Index